You Call This Living?

You Call This Living?

A Collection of East European Political Jokes

C. Banc and Alan Dundes

The University of Georgia Press
Athens and London

© 1990 by Alan Dundes
Athens, Georgia 30602
All rights reserved
Set in Times Roman
The paper in this book meets the guidelines for
permanence and durability of the Committee on
Production Guidelines for Book Longevity of the
Council on Library Resources.

Printed in the United States of America
94   93   92   91   90   5   4   3   2
Library of Congress Cataloging in Publication Data
Banc, C.
    [First prize, fifteen years!]
    You call this living? : a collection of East European political
jokes / C. Banc and Alan Dundes.
        p.   cm.
    "First published by Fairleigh Dickinson University Press in 1986
as First prize, fifteen years!"—T.p. verso.
    Includes bibliographical references and index.
    ISBN 0-8203-1282-7 (alk. paper). — ISBN 0-8203-1283-5 (pbk:
alk. paper)
    1. Communism—Humor. 2. Political satire, Romanian—Transla-
tions into English. 3. Political satire, English—Translations from
Romanian. 4. Europe, Eastern—Politics and government—Humor.
I. Dundes, Alan. II. Title.
PN6231.C612B28   1990
818'.5402—dc20   90-39416   CIP

British Library Cataloging in Publication Data available

First published by Fairleigh Dickinson University
Press as *First Prize: Fifteen Years!*
© 1986 by Associated University Presses, Inc.

To the memory of CB's father
Who told jokes as few could.

Contents

Preface

In mid-December 1989, the following joke circulated in Czechoslovakia: What's the difference between eastern Europe and the United States of America? The answer: The United States of America still has a Communist party.

The joke reflected something of the enormous number of unheralded political changes sweeping across the Soviet bloc. To the outside observer, it seemed akin to a domino effect as one eastern European country after another indulged in mass crowd demonstrations that successfully toppled the governments in power. Historians will have to determine just when and where these truly remarkable events started. Did they begin in Poland with the rise of a strong trade union of shipyard workers called Solidarity? Were the events encouraged by the new Soviet leader, Gorbachev, who made it clear that the U.S.S.R. would not intervene to support a communist government in trouble? To the world's amazement, the demise of communism was accomplished with relative calm in East Germany, Czechoslovakia, and Hungary.

Only in Romania was there bloodshed as the tyrant Nicolae Ceausescu ordered the Securitate, his dreaded secret police, to shoot fellow Romanians, citizen demonstrators in the streets of the city of Timisoara in the far western part of Romania (Nelan, 1990). They did so on December 16 and 17, 1989—violence that led ultimately to the ouster of Ceausescu. After his capture on December 22, he and his equally hated wife Elena were given a sham two-hour secret trial on Christmas day. Later that day, the couple was executed by firing squad. Though the international community deplored the lack of a proper, duly constituted trial, it was more or less understood that the revolutionaries wished to eliminate any possibility that Ceausescu loyalists would attempt a countercoup to reinstate the regime.

In Romania and elsewhere in eastern Europe, not only was the reigning communist government forced by public pressure to resign from power, but there were concerted efforts to ban the very existence of the

Communist party in several countries. This tendency was nicely articulated in a Hungarian joke dating from September 1989 (anon., 1989b): Do you know what prizes the Communists are now offering for recruiting new party members? If you get one new member, you don't pay dues. Two new members, you can quit the party. And for three, you get a certificate saying you were never a member.

It is precisely this kind of pointed political joke that was the subject of our book *First Prize: Fifteen Years!*, originally published in 1986 and now reprinted in this new edition. Although the entire corpus of more than three hundred jokes came from a Romanian oral source, the comparative notes make it clear that the jokes belonged to eastern Europe or the Soviet bloc as a whole. There is no question that the jokes contained in this collection were told and retold throughout eastern Europe as well as in the Soviet Union—hence the new title, *You Call This Living? A Collection of East European Political Jokes.* We present Romanian versions of jokes that have long been a part of the humor repertoire in Poland, Czechoslovakia, Hungary, East Germany, Bulgaria, Yugoslavia, and Albania, among other countries.

The interest in political jokes in the past decade or so seems to have intensified. Many collections of political jokes—some large, some small—have appeared in print, often in relatively obscure newsletters. We find, for example, discussions of political jokes from Iran (Radhayrapetian, 1983; Carnes, 1989); from the Arab world (Kishtainy, 1985), especially Egypt (Lutfi al-Sayyid Marsot, 1980; Webber, 1987); from Spain (Brandes, 1977), Mexico (Beezley, 1985), Cuba (anon., 1989a), and the Philippines (Rafael, 1986); and from the Soviet Union (Shturman and Tictin, 1985; Ruksenas, 1986; Harris and Rabinovich, 1988; and Harris, 1989). Eastern Europe was not neglected: we find collections covering the area in general (Engel, 1984) as well as individual countries—East Germany (Stein, 1989), for example, and especially Romania (Mavrodin, 1983; Popescu, 1985; Cochran, 1989). There are also more specialized studies such as those probing the origins of the political joke (Benton, 1988), political jokes in Nazi Germany (Torberg, 1967), or the Radio Erevan joke cycle (Hellberg, 1985).

In reviewing these materials, we can see that some political jokes are easily transferable to any dictatorship but others are peculiar to particular regimes. For example, a joke told in Iran (Radhayrapetian, 1983) during the time the Ayatollah Khomeini was in power would not necessarily apply to all totalitarian states: "As the plane approached Iran, the passengers aboard heard the captain saying, 'Ladies and gentlemen, this is your captain speaking. We are now flying over Iran and will be landing soon. Please turn your watches back a hundred years.'"

The majority of political joke compilations are totally devoid of any accompanying commentary or analysis. This anti-intellectual stance is sometimes even cited as a cause for self-congratulation: "We do not here commit the crime of killing our jokes with explanations. Nor do we come to bury them in footnotes: a joke in need of a footnote is a dead joke" (Lukes and Galnoor, 1985:xii). Although some jokes may be intelligible cross-culturally, others are more subtle and so enmeshed in their culture that they cannot be understood without the aid of a native *explication de texte*. We much prefer our own strategy. In preparing the first edition, if we felt a joke could be understood without commentary we tried not to belabor the obvious; but if we thought it would be meaningless without inside knowledge of the cultural nuances it reflected, we did not hesitate to provide necessary background information. See, for example, the joke in our collection concerning a car owner found dead with traces of yogurt in his stomach (pp. 102–3). We make no apology for our explanations, because we feel that many live jokes are dead outside of their immediate cultural context and that a single informative footnote may well bring a dead joke to life.

After some deliberation, we have decided not to alter the main body of this volume. We believe that the jokes and their commentary stand as a reliable record of regimes that we trust are now safely part of the past. The many jokes purporting to tell, for example, of Ceausescu's death (Cochran, 1989) are no longer needed, as fiction has turned into fact and wishful thinking into reality. If we are right about the basic function of these political jokes—to serve as a vital communal defense mechanism in a time of severe totalitarian repression—then the removal of the governments responsible for such repression should eliminate the need for such jokes. If, on the other hand, the peoples of eastern Europe are unable to enjoy their newly won freedoms because some other form of repressive government comes to power, one would expect the political joke tradition to continue. Naturally, we hope that such jokes will *not* be needed in the future.

It was tempting to consider adding more commentary to individual jokes contained in our original corpus. There is the joke, for example, in which different philosophies are likened to chasing a black cat in a dark room (pp. 70–71). We traced parallels back to 1961. In his memoirs written originally in 1927, however, Finnish anthropologist Edward Westermarck recalled from his study of philosophy in the 1880s a definition of a philosopher as "a blind man in a pitch-dark room looking for a black hat that is not there at all" (1929:30). One wonders if this eminent scholar might possibly have misheard the English words "black cat"; in any case, the joke is clearly much older than we had initially indicated. Another joke that may have much earlier antecedents is one in which the K.G.B. digs up a man's garden in search of hidden gold coins (p. 39). One reviewer (Belgrader, 1989:112) aptly suggested that this may be a modern-day variant of Aarne-Thompson tale type 910E, Father's Counsel: Where Treasure Is, a tale which goes back at least to an Aesopic fable.

With respect to finding older sources for our political jokes, we are gratified that one of our texts—a joke in which an animal or man flees because of a decree threatening to shoot all camels (pp. 33–34)—has become the subject of an interesting scholarly debate. Omidsalar (1987) cited several medieval Persian texts of the joke, the earliest dating from the twelfth century. In one a fox fears a king's order that all donkeys are to be taken for forced labor, while in another it is a man rather than a fox who believes he will be taken for an ass. However, Marzolph (1988) proposed an Arabic instead of an Iranian source, citing eleventh- and tenth-century texts. In both texts, a camel runs away because donkeys or mules are being pressed into service. From our perspective, it is significant that the twentieth-century Romanian political joke we reported goes back at least one thousand years and that through the astonishing continuity of oral tradition the very same animal mentioned in our text—the camel—is involved as a character in the oldest Arabic versions of the joke.

For most of the jokes in our collection, there would be little to add to the annotation. To be sure, some new versions have appeared in the anthologies (cited above) that were published after our book first appeared; but inasmuch as the search for parallels is essentially an endless task, we did not think it worthwhile to reset the entire book just to add one or two more parallels to several dozen texts. Another temptation was to add more jokes to our original compilation. Political jokes continued to flourish in Romania right up to the overthrow of Ceausescu in late 1989. But again we decided not to reset the book for the sake of a half-dozen or so new texts. Some of these jokes are quite interesting, particularly those illustrating eastern European emphases different from concerns expressed in internationally distributed political jokes. In the late 1980s, for example, the following joke circulated in the United States: A sociological man-in-the-street poll was taken in four countries in each of which the same question was posed: "Excuse me, sir, what is your opinion of the recently announced shortage of meat?" In Poland, a man in downtown Warsaw asked, "What is meat?" In the United States, a man in Texas asked "What is shortage?" In the Soviet Union, a man in Moscow asked, "What is opinion?" Finally, in Israel, a man in Tel Aviv asked, "What is 'Excuse me'?"

In other versions of this joke, what is stereotypically perceived as aggressive rudeness in Israeli behavior is not present (cf. Cuban and Mexican versions [anon., 1989a:3; Beezley 1985:215]). We may compare a Romanian version of the joke collected between 1985 and 1987 (Cochran, 1989:272): "A Russian dog, a Polish dog, and a Romanian dog meet to discuss plans for celebrating the New Year. 'We could have the party at my place,' suggests the Russian dog. 'I've got some meat, but we can't bark.' The Polish dog then suggests his home. 'There isn't any meat,' he says, 'but it's OK to bark.' Meanwhile the Romanian dog looks more and more puzzled. Finally he speaks. 'What's meat?' he asks. 'What's barking?'" This Romanian version suggests that the plight of Romania—where neither food nor free speech can be found—is worse than that of other Socialist countries. (The barking metaphor for freedom of speech strongly suggests another standard eastern European joke; see pp. 32–33.)

Some readers of the earlier edition of our book asserted that we had exaggerated the terrible conditions of life in Romania under Ceausescu's dictatorial rule and elsewhere in eastern Europe, claiming that it could not possibly be so bleak and miserable as we indicated. Yet in the aftermath of the physical removal of Ceausescu, the facts reveal that the jokes we reported told the truth. One joke (pp. 100–102), for example, commented through a series of drawings upon Ceausescu's policy against birth control. Television interviews with Romanian women revealed the devastating effects of this policy. It became clear that for years women had been forced against their will to give birth and that Romanian orphanages were overcrowded with unwanted children.

We fervently hope that the 1989 revolution in Romania and comparable changes in other eastern European countries will put an end to the horrors of nearly forty-five years of socialist tyranny. Time will tell whether that is the case. If so, the conditions that created or encouraged the jokes in this volume will disappear without regret and the jokes will serve as a reminder of the deplorable conditions that once prevailed behind the Iron Curtain. It cannot be stated too strongly that these jokes provide a unique historical record of the living conditions that the peoples of eastern Europe were forced to endure for many decades. They show how fragile and difficult life under political oppression can be. If, on the other hand, by some ill stroke of luck a "new" Ceausescu should come to power in Romania or in some other country of eastern Europe these same jokes will no doubt resurface in updated form to reflect whatever political realities may come to pass.

Either way, the jokes constitute an important part of modern eastern European folklore.

The title of this new edition evokes the lamentable living conditions that prevailed for so long in eastern Europe. It comes from a standard joke (p. 164; cf. Engel, 1984:78, and Ruksenas, 1986:72) in which a man knocks at the door of a humble dwelling on the outskirts of Bucharest. An old man sticks his head out of the window, whereupon the following dialogue takes place:

—Does the tailor Rabinowitch live here?
—No.
—Who are you?
—Rabinowitch.
—And aren't you a tailor?
—Yes, I am.
—Then why did you say you didn't live here?
—You call this living?

Acknowledgments

We thank the countless anonymous creators of political jokes and also those who dare to keep them alive by transmitting them. We also appreciate the assistance of Veronika Görög-Karady in Paris and especially Renate Vollmer in Frankfort for sending us important collections of political jokes published in France and Germany.

You Call This Living?

1
Introduction

When God created man, he gave him three qualities: to be honest, to be clever, and to be communist. Then came the devil who decided that this was too much. A man should have only two of the three qualities, in any combination—a man can be either honest and communist, but then he is not clever; or clever and communist, but then he is not honest; or clever and honest, but then he is not a communist.

For East German versions, see Dor and Federmann, 1964:152, and Brandt, 1965:127; for a Czech version, Paruit, 1978:141. For other versions, Durocher, 1965:102; Hirche, 1977:136. This joke, like a number of others in this collection, can be traced back to comparable, if not identical, texts circulating in Nazi Germany. For example, an Englishman was asked after a visit to Germany how he found Germans. He answered that they are honest, intelligent and National Socialist, but unfortunately these three qualities never occurred together. Any one German had only two of them. Either he is honest and intelligent but then he is not a National Socialist, or he is intelligent and a National Socialist but then he is not honest, or he is honest and a National Socialist but then he is not intelligent. See Gamm, 1979[1963]:12. Another joke which plays upon the alleged incompatibility of communism and intellectual honesty occurs in question form: Who is a Communist? He who has read all the works of Marx and Lenin. And who is an anti-Communist? He who understands their works. See Drozdzynski, 1974:92; Melor, 1979:126; and Kalina, 1980:82. For the full bibliographical citations to references mentioned in the comparative notes to the jokes, consult the bibliography at the end of this volume.

At the sixtieth anniversary of the October Revolution, a huge meeting is held in Red Square. Brezhnev's speech:

—Comrades, we are now celebrating the sixtieth anniversary of our great revolution. Comrades, when we say "Revolution," we mean Lenin! When we say "Lenin," we mean the Communist party! When we say "Communist party," we mean class struggle! When we say "class struggle," we mean the working class which for centuries has led this struggle . . . and so, comrades, for the last sixty years we keep saying one thing and meaning something else!

For another version, see Kolasky, 1972:86.

Question:
—Are the extraordinary achievements of communism known all over the world?
Answer:
—In principle, yes, but unfortunately this is communism's greatest handicap.

One of the most popular joke cycles behind the Iron Curtain takes the format of question and answer. Typically, the question is addressed to Radio Erevan, the radio station in Soviet Armenia. Radio Erevan jokes are known and enjoyed throughout eastern Europe and the Soviet Union. Quite a number of the previously published collections of political jokes from this part of the world are specifically Radio Erevan joking questions. Inevitably, the naive Radio Erevan speaks the truth albeit unwittingly. It has been suggested that the question-and-answer jokes attributed to Radio Erevan are but a modern updating of older "Armenian" stories popular all over eastern Europe before World War I (Langnas 1963:17). In the Soviet Union, the jokes are told with a sham Armenian accent (Kalbouss 1977:448). For examples of Radio Erevan jokes, see Sulzberger, 1962; Schiff, 1969, 1975; Parth and Schiff, 1972; Olin, 1970; Steiger, 1976; and Kalbouss, 1977.

The joke above does belong to the Radio Erevan cycle. For a parallel, see Schiff, 1969:63, Melor, 1979:99, 222. There are numerous jokes about the boasting of Communists. For example, in a Polish text, a little boy, Piotr, is asked by his teacher what makes the Communist system superior to others. He responds, "Communism is superior because it adequately copes with difficulties which do not exist in other systems." See LoBello, 1966:23. For other versions, see Streit, 1964:56, Durocher, 1965:71; Kolasky, 1972:63; and Hirche, 1977:131.

—Father, is it true that those who invented communism were scientists?
—Yes, son, it's true.
—Why, then, didn't they try it first on laboratory animals?

For other Romanian versions (Were Karl Marx and Friedrich Engels true scientists? No, if they had been true scientists, they would have tried out socialism first on animals.) see Drozdzynski, 1974:204, and Jacobi, 1965:129. For Polish versions, see anon., 1969b:25, and Isnard, 1977:27. For other versions, see Durocher, 1965:179–180; Swoboda, 1969:34; anon., 1977:671; Paruit, 1978:186; Kalina, 1980:76; and Dolgopolova, 1982:81.

At a nursery school the children have just finished singing together a hymn in praise of the party. Now the teacher chats with them and Ionel tells her:
—I have a cat, and she just had six kittens, and all of them are communist.
The teacher is very pleased and proud that her efforts in indoctrination have yielded such good results. Next day when an inspector comes to visit the nursery, she asks Ionel to tell his story again.
—I have a cat, and she had six kittens, and four of them are communist.
—But yesterday you said that all of them were communist, says the teacher.
—Yes, says Ionel, but two of them have opened their eyes.

In an interesting Romanian variant, six little red kittens are born. The party officials are delighted. A deputy goes to the farmhouse where he finds the kittens are white. How can that be, he asks. The farmer explains: while they were blind, they were red, but now that they have opened their eyes, they have become white. See Drozdzynski, 1974:204–5; For a version of the joke set in Bulgaria, see Streit, 1964:28; for a Polish version, see Lo Bello, 1966:23; for an East German version, see Brandt, 1965:105; for another version (with puppies instead of kittens), see Paruit, 1978:182. This joke goes back to Nazi times. For a 1934 text describing seven kittens, see Hirche, 1964:114–15.

2
The Reign of Terror

—*A competition for the best political joke was announced. Do you know what the first prize was?*
—*No.*
—*Fifteen years.*

This appears to be an updating of an older joke. A German version offers a first prize of twenty years in Dachau! (Röhrich, 1977:211). A Russian version from 1949 enumerated different penalties depending upon the subject of the joke: the late President Kalinin, five years; Molotov, eight years; and Stalin, ten years (Dallin, 1949:15). For additional Russian versions, see Dor and Federmann, 1964:215 (twenty years); and Draitser, 1978:29 (twenty-five years). For a Czech version (ten years forced labor), see Beckmann, 1969:12; for a version set in Yugoslavia where the competition involves jokes about Tito (twenty years), see Meyer, 1978:110. For other versions of this popular joke, see Hirche, 1964:280 (twenty years); Brandt, 1965:90 (twenty years); Durocher, 1965:53 (twenty-five years hard labor); Benton and Loomes, 1976:120 (twenty years); Isnard, 1977:15 (twenty-five years in a psychiatric clinic); Paruit, 1978:18 (twenty years); Melor, 1979:136 (twenty years); and Larsen, 1980:88 (twenty years in a labor camp).

—*Do you know who built the left bank of the Danube Canal?*
—*No.*
—*The people who told this joke. And do you know who built the right bank?*
—*No.*
—*The people who listened to this joke and didn't report it.*

For other versions, see Kolasky, 1972: vii, and Kalina, 1980: 59. In a related text, two friends meet on a street. One tells the other a political joke. The second persons says, "I arrest you. You have just told an anti-Soviet joke." The first retorts, "and I arrest you too. You listened to it all the way through." See Paruit, 1978: 38, and Kalina, 1980: 58. For a Nazi parallel, see Gamm, 1979[1963]: 26.

The importance of political jokes in the Iron Curtain countries is signalled by the existence of jokes about these jokes. For example, "Why are there so many jokes about communism?" "Because no one takes it seriously." Kalina, 1980: 229. Or "When will the promised Paradise on earth prevail in Hungary?" "When industrial and agricultural productivity reach the production level of political jokes." Kalina, 1980: 116. It is safest not to tell such jokes. In one text, a prosecuting attorney visits one of his friends, a state judge. He sees him reading a document in his office, doubled over with laughter. "What is making you laugh like that?" "An absolutely fantastic political joke!" "Tell it." "No . . . I just gave five years for it." Melor, 1979: 137.

In a labor camp.
—What are you here for?
—Laziness.
—You mean you didn't fulfill your plan?
—No. After a conversation on some political issues with a colleague, I put off denouncing him until the next day, but he didn't.

For other versions, see Durocher, 1965: 61; Drozdzynski, 1974: 50; Benton and Loomes, 1976: 130; and Melor, 1979: 132. It is difficult for Americans and other westerners to comprehend the climate of fear caused by not knowing who among one's circle of friends, even close friends, might be serving as an informer. A "friend" or former colleague may suddenly turn up as principal accuser. A Hungarian text illustrates this point: "The Hungarian Secret Police arrested two citizens but shortly afterward released one of them. Before the freed man left the station, he managed to ask the one who was detained, "What did you confess to?" "I confessed I bought sugar on the black market." "Why did you confess it, for heaven's sake?" "I couldn't help it; the man who interrogated me had sold me the sugar." See "No Recourse," *News from Behind the Iron Curtain* 3, no. 7 (July, 1954): 45. A variant, also from Hungary, shows how former fascists have become zealous communists: "The A.V.H. arrested two gypsies, called in one for questioning and told the other one to wait outside. Several hours passed. Suddenly the door opened and the first gypsy fell out at his friend's feet. The friend asked: "Did you tell the A.V.H. that you used to play music for the Fascists? Is that why they beat you up?" "I had no choice," replied the first gypsy. "I was questioned by the same Fascists that I used to play music for." See Luray, 1957:16. For another version from Hungary, see Jacobi, 1965:9; for another version, see Paruit, 1978:69.

While waiting for the bus at an overcrowded bus stop, Ionescu starts a conversation with a stranger. A beautiful Chevrolet races by.
—That Volga is really beautiful, isn't it?
The stranger doesn't answer. After a while, a Mercedes passes by and Ionescu exclaims:
—Oh, look at that beautiful Zil.
Now the stranger can't stand it any longer.
—You don't seem to know very much about cars, he says.
—I know a lot about cars, it's you I know nothing about.

Volga and Zil are Soviet-made cars. For an earlier Romanian version, see Dundes, 1971:51–52; for Czech versions, see Kukin, 1962:[140]; Dor and Federmann, 1964:256; Drozdzynski, 1974:153; Benton and Loomes, 1976:113; Isnard, 1977:54; Beckmann, 1980:16; and Larsen, 1980:102. For versions set in East Germany, see Brandt, 1965:67, and Hirche, 1977:196; for a version set in Yugoslavia, see Meyer, 1978:111; for a Hungarian version, see Jacobi, 1965:3. For another version, see Streit, 1964:56. It is of interest that the earliest version of the above was reported in Mischka Kukin's 1962 collection *Humor hinter dem Eisernen Vorhang.* Kukin, according to Levy (1976:22), is a pseudonym for famed Nazi-hunter Simon Wiesenthal. He supposedly published his major collection of political jokes under a nom de plume in order to protect his serious image in the West and to keep his lines of communication open to authorities in the eastern block.

Two Romanians are on a bus. One is sitting down; the other is standing. The man sitting asks:
—Are you a member of the Communist party?
—No, I am not.

—*Are you in the military?*
—*No, I am not.*
—*You mean you are not a government or party official of any kind?*
—*No, I am not.*
—*Then get the hell off my foot!*

For versions set in Russia, see Meyer, 1978:120; Paruit, 1978:41; Melor, 1979:155; and Kalina, 1980:41. For a version set in Portugal, see Benton and Loomes, 1976:71–72; for a modern Greek version, see Orso, 1979:17.

Two friends meet on the street.
—*How are you, how's everything?*
—*Not bad at all. I've got a good job and a nice position in the party, my wife is in the women's organization and also has a nice job, my kids are in school and both are satisfied with their activities in the communist youth group . . .*
—*Say, Ilie, what do you think you're doing? Are you talking to me in person or over the telephone?*

During the Stalinist years.
Ilie is lying in bed, fast asleep. At four o'clock in the morning, a loud knock on his door wakes him up. He stares at the door, paralyzed with fear.
—*It's all right, Ilie, shouts his neighbor, don't worry, it's only me. All I wanted to tell you is that your house is on fire.*

For an earlier Romanian version, see Dor and Federmann, 1964:275; for Russian versions, see Wolfe, 1951:13; Draitser, 1978:33; and Dolgopolova, 1982:33; for a Hungarian version, see Sanders, 1962:25; for a Czech version, see Kalina, 1980:63; for East German versions, see Hirche, 1964:245; Brandt, 1965:95; and Adolph Schalk, *The Germans* (Englewood Cliffs, N.J.: Prentice-Hall, 1971), 65; for other versions, see Winick, 1964:35; Drozdyznski, 1974:40; Benton and Loomes, 1976:138–39; Paruit, 1978:35; and Melor, 1979:143. In an interesting variant, a family is awakened in the middle of the night by some noise in the apartment. Everyone keeps silent as they are petrified with fear. Finally a voice whispers, "Relax, it is only a thief." Durocher, 1965:62.

A Romanian of German origin applies to emigrate to West Germany.
—Why do you want to leave the country in which you were born?
asks the passport officer. You have a good position here, a large apart-
ment. Do you expect to find better conditions in Germany?
—Oh, no. But what bothers me here is the milkman. Every morning
he wakes me up at six with a loud bang on my door.
—But if you want your milk brought to your door, won't the same
thing happen in Germany, too?
—Yes, but there I'll know it's only the milkman.

For a Czech version, see Beckmann, 1969:61, and Larsen, 1980:36.
For other versions, see Benton and Loomes, 1976:136–37, and Paruit,
1978:33. For a version told in Nazi Germany, see Gamm,
1979[1963]:15.

—Is there any advantage in a one-party system?
—In principle, yes. It would be so much more complicated to watch
out not to say or do anything wrong if there were several parties.

For another version, see Schiff, 1969:68. This joke is reminiscent of
a Hungarian text, "Why is the sale of liquor prohibited during the
Hungarian elections? So that no one should see two parties where
there is only one. See *News from Behind the Iron Curtain,* 2, no. 7
(July, 1953): 60.

An American correspondent in Moscow wants to know what the man
on the street really thinks about domestic and international issues. He
stops a man at random, engages in small talk with him, and then asks:
—What do you think about the Middle East conflict?
—Well, I read what Pravda *writes on this matter, and I agree with it.*
—What's your opinion on the Russian economy?
—I read yesterday the economics column in Izvestia *and I quite*
agree with it.
—What about the state of Soviet agriculture?
—There's an article today in the Agricultural Gazette *about it. I*
agree with it.
The American loses patience:
—But man, Haven't you got an opinion of your own?
—Sure I have. But I don't agree with it.

For a Czech version, see Filip and Steiger, 1977:24. For another version, see Benton and Loomes, 1976:134.

A group of friends travel together in a train compartment. An outsider is intrigued to see that each time one of them mentions a number, all the others roll with laughter. He finally asks for an explanation, but does not get one. At the next station, another man joins the group, and the new man knows the outsider well.

—He's all right, pals, we may tell him. The fact is that we all know a large number of political jokes, but since for obvious reasons we cannot tell them in the presence of an outsider, we have assigned a number to each joke. Each number brings to our minds the joke it stands for, and that's why we're laughing.

The outsider wants to try it, too.

—Forty-five, he says, at random.

But no one laughs. He looks inquiringly at his friend.

—Well, it's not the joke, it's the way you tell it.

This joke is well known in the West, but it has a different significance in the eastern European setting. The implication is that "the way you tell it" includes an appropriate occasion for the joke. In other words, it is not the joke, but *when* you tell it. For a brief discussion of an American version of telling jokes by the numbers, see Alan Dundes, "Defining Identity through Folklore," in Anita Jacobson-Widding, ed., *Identity: Personal and Socio-Cultural: A Symposium,* Uppsala Studies in Cultural Anthropology 5 (Uppsala, 1983), 258–59.

—How do people of different nationalities react upon hearing a joke?

—An Englishman laughs three times: when he hears the joke, when he remembers it, and when he understands it. A German laughs twice: when he hears the joke, and when he remembers it, for in any case, he will never understand it. A Frenchman laughs once, when he hears it. A Jew never laughs, because he already knows the joke.

—And a Romanian?

—He laughs only once: when he gets promoted for having informed on his colleague who told the joke.

For a version of this joke common in the West, see Alan Dundes, "A Study of Ethnic Slurs: The Jew and the Polack in the United States,"

Journal of American Folklore 84 (1971): 191. For another version, see Irving Howe, "The Nature of Jewish Laughter," *American Mercury* 72 (1961): 211–12.

An Englishman: A gentleman.
Two Englishmen: A club.
Three Englishmen: A colony.

A Frenchman: Un homme d'esprit [a man of wit].
Two Frenchmen: Une grande nation [a great nation].
Three Frenchmen: Un mariage [a marriage].

A Romanian: A loafer.
Two Romanians: A clique.
Three Romanians: A clique plus an informer.

This is a standard form of *blason populaire* or national/ethnic slur. For example, a German variant contrasts French and Germans as follows:

One Frenchman is a vagabond.
Two Frenchmen is love.
Three Frenchmen is a marriage.

One German is a philosopher.
Two Germans is an organization.
Three Germans is war.

See Alan Dundes, "Slurs International: Folk Comparisons of Ethnicity and National Character," *Southern Folklore Quarterly* 39 (1975): 26. For a Polish version which speaks only of Germans: One German—a beer; two Germans—an organization; three Germans—a war, see Abraham Roback, *A Dictionary of International Slurs* (Cambridge, Mass., 1944), 172. For an elaborate text of this type which treats nine different national groups, see Hirche, 1977:94–95. For another version, see Dolgopolova, 1982:52. For a French text, see Gamm, 1979[1963]:41.

A question for Radio Erevan.
—Is it true that divorce is difficult to obtain in the Soviet Union?

—In principle yes, but divorce is unnecessary in our country. When a person wants to get rid of his (her) partner, all he has to do is to inform on him (her) to the K.G.B.

For another version, see Kolasky, 1972:121.

Mitica is summoned to the party committee.
—We've heard that you have become a religious fanatic.
—Me, comrade? Impossible.
—There's no use denying it. We know positively that every morning you make the sign of the cross.
—Oh, no comrades, what I actually do is this: each morning before leaving home, I touch my forehead and say to myself, Mitica, watch what you say. Then I check to see if I have buttoned my pants. Then I touch my breast pocket to make sure I have my party membership card. Then I pat myself on the right shoulder and say to myself, Good boy, Mitica!

This is a standard joke in the West told about a Jew who is accused of acting like a Catholic. In the punchline, he explains that he is simply checking "spectacles, testicles, etc." For a representative text, see Blanche Knott, *Truly Tasteless Jokes Three* (New York: Ballantine Books, 1983), 92–93.

At home Mitica is looking in the mirror and says:
—Now look here, Mitica, which of us two is the informer?

The number of Romanian political jokes mentioning informers does attest to the prevalence of this terrible practice. In a remarkable commentary on both the practice and the joke telling it inspires, we find an Englishman, German, and a Russian were arguing about which nation was the bravest. The Englishman claimed the English are the bravest because one in every ten is drowned at sea. The German protested that Germans are the bravest because one in every six dies on the battlefield. "You are both wrong," said the Russian. "*We* are the bravest, because even though every second one of us is an informer, we still tell political jokes." See Benton and Loomes, 1976:85.

In Bucharest in 1950 a man looks at a picture of Stalin in a shop window and mumbles, "Swine, swine, swine." Two men from the security police arrest him on the spot.
—Who are you calling swine?
—Why, Churchill, of course, who is giving such a hard time to our beloved Stalin.
—Who are you trying to fool? Don't you think we know who the swine is?

For an earlier version in which dog rather than swine is used, see Kukin, 1962:[12]. For another version (about Brezhnev and Nixon), see Paruit, 1978:47. For a version from Nazi Germany (also about Churchill) see Gamm, 1979[1963]:31. For another version (about Americans and Russians in general), see Melor, 1979:135. In a variant, a Russian worker walking along the street with a friend exclaims, "It's a rotten government." A guard seizes him and places him under arrest. The worker asks, "What for?" The guard explains, "Because you said it is a rotten government." The citizen protested, "But I never said what government." "No good," replied the guard. "There is only one rotten government and you know it." See Winick, 1964:32.

Two Romanian policemen were standing on guard together. One asked the other:
—What do you think of our regime?
—The same as you.
—In that case, it is my duty to arrest you.

For an older Austrian version involving standard joke cycle figure Count Bobbi (Graf Bobby) and his solicited opinion of the Third Reich, see Dor and Federmann, 1964:186. For an East German text, see Hirche, 1964:240, who comments that this is a standard joke for all political systems in which free speech is forbidden or dangerous, and he remarks further that it was told in Nazi times. For other East German versions, see Brandt, 1965:203, and Kolasky, 1972:33. For versions set in Hungary, see "Sure Giveaway," *East Europe,* 6, no. 2 (February, 1957), 24, and Aranyossy, 1971:100–101. For Czech versions, see Swoboda, 1969:23; Paruit, 1978:55; for a Russian version, see Isnard, 1977:76–77. For other versions, see Durocher, 1965:56, and Melor, 1979:129.

A man is brought into court, accused of having dangerous ideas.
—What did he say? asks the judge.
—Owing to the vigilance of our secret police, he was arrested before
he could say anything, answers the prosecutor.

For other versions, see Winick, 1964:40, and Kolasky, 1972:73.

Two men are exchanging political jokes, which, like many jokes in
Romania, begin with the formula "What's the difference between . . ."
A man joins the group and after listening for a while asks:
—And do you know what the difference is between a watch and you?
—No.
—The watch walks (runs) by itself, and you (showing his secret police
badge) walk with me.

In a variant, two friends are speaking loudly in a cafe. One asks the other if he knows the difference between Stalin and Brezhnev. The other says no. The first says there is no difference because neither one of them understood anything about Marxism. At that point, someone in civilian clothes rises from a nearby table and asks them, "Do you know the difference between a day and you?" "No," the two say. "Well, the days follow one another and are not alike whereas you are going to follow me please." See Paruit, 1978:29. In another variant, a different unit of time is employed. The joke ends, "Do you know the difference between the twelve months and you?" "No." "The months follow one another and come around again while you will now follow me and come around no more." See Kalina, 1980:60. In still another variant, two friends meet in a tramway in Warsaw. One poses a riddle to the other, "What is the difference between a napkin and the government?" The friend cannot answer so the first explains, "The napkin is used to wipe the mouth and the government is just right for wiping the ass." Thereupon a third passenger enters the game and asks, "And what is the difference between you and the conductor?" The two friends have no response. Then the strangers shows his card of police inspector and declares, "The conductor will go to the end of the line and you, you will get off with me at the next stop." Immediately, the author of the first riddle protests. He was in no way thinking, he said, of the Polish government. "Sir," replied the policeman, "I have served with the police for fifteen years and I am well placed to be someone to know which government is just right for wiping the ass." See Durocher, 1965:63–64.

It is October 1944. A man comes to a police station to make a complaint.
—Two Swiss soldiers have looted my house and raped my wife and daughter.
—What do you mean, Swiss soldiers? There isn't a single Swiss soldier in Romania.
—I tell you they were Swiss soldiers.
—Think again. Weren't they perhaps Russian soldiers?
—You said it, sir, not me.

For a Polish version dated 1945, see Drozdzynski, 1974:110. For other Polish versions, see Kukin, 1962:[120], and Brandt, 1965:10–11. For a Czech version in which a German tourist reports to a Prague policeman that three Swiss stole his Soviet watch, see Filip and Steiger, 1977:39. For additional Czech versions, see Hirche, 1977:166; Meyer, 1978:100; Paruit, 1978:136; Kalina, 1980:219; and Larsen, 1980:101. For other versions, see Benton and Loomes, 1976:109–10, and Isnard, 1977:35. It seems more than likely that this joke is an updating of a standard European folktale, namely tale type 925, Tidings brought to the King: You said it, not I. See Antti Aarne and Stith Thompson, *The Types of the Folktale,* 2d revision (Helsinki, 1961). Although jokes constitute a major segment of the Aarne-Thompson tale typology (types 1200–1999), political jokes are not included. This confirms the fact that political jokes have been neglected by folklorists.

Question:
—Should we abolish the entire informer system?
Answer:
—In principle, yes, but how would we deal with all the millions of unemployed?

For another version, see Schiff, 1969:96.

A dog crosses the Hungarian border to Austria. An Austrian dog asks him:

—Why did you do this? Are the bones better here than in Hungary?
—No, but here I can bark.

In a Russian version, a French, an English, and a Russian dog all run away to Switzerland. The French dog complains that only the rich in France can afford to enjoy life while the English dog claims that British austerity got him down. The Russian dog says, "We have plenty of everything, plenty to eat, plenty to wear—but I do feel like barking now and then, too." See Dallin, 1949:15. For another version involving Polish and Czech dogs—the Polish dog goes to Czechoslovakia for something to eat; the Czech dog goes to Poland in order to bark—, see "Aesop on the Border," *East Europe,* 7, no. 7 (July, 1958): 16. For other Czech versions, see Kukin, 1962:[140]; Beckmann, 1969:49; Swoboda, 1969:33–34; Schiff, 1975:28; and Kalina, 198:243. For a Bulgarian version, see Lo Bello, 1966:25; for a Polish version, see Levy, 1976:25. In an East German variant, two dachshunds meet at a crossing point. One is from West Berlin and one from East Berlin. "How goes it over there?" asks the West dog. "Prima [first rate]," answers the East dog. "So why did you come over?" For once I would simply like to bark." Brandt, 1965:87. For another East German text, see Hirche, 1964:246–47, who claims that this joke was told in the Nazi era as well. In a Russian version, the protagonists are French and Soviet sparrows. The latter explains that although there is grain on the roads, it is "bursting to be allowed to sing . . ." Dolgopolova, 1982:31.

A man is running in panic down a Bucharest street. A friend stops him.
—Why are you running like this?
—Didn't you hear? They have decided to shoot all camels.
—But for heaven's sake, you're not a camel.
—Yes, but these people shoot first, and then they realize you're not a camel!

For other versions of this extremely popular joke, see Wolfe, 1951:13 (rabbits); Winick, 1964:58 (camels); Durocher, 1965:177–78 (rabbits); Kolasky, 1972:71–72 (rabbits); Benton and Loomes, 1976:87 (giraffes); Isnard, 1977:78–79 (bears); Draitser, 1978:23 (rabbits); Meyer, 1978:110 (rabbits); Paruit, 1978:31 (cats); Melor, 1979:143 (rabbits); and Kalina, 1980:65 (dogs). Draitser claims the text dates from 1937. In a version current in Nazi Germany, countless rabbits appeared one day at the Belgian border explaining they were political refugees. "The Gestapo is arresting all giraffes as enemies of the state." "But you are not giraffes." "We know that, but try to make that clear to a member of the Gestapo." See Gamm, 1979[1963]:20. Actually, during the Nazi occupation of Romania, there was another version:

> There is a decree ordering that anyone who has more than two testicles shall have his testicles cut off. A man is running down the street and is stopped by a friend. He tells the friend of the decree.
> —Come on, you certainly don't have more than two.
> —Yes, but these people cut them off first, and then they count them.

For references to Jewish variants of this general joke type, including several told in czarist times, see Dov Noy, ed., *Folktales of Israel* (Chicago: University of Chicago Press, 1963), pp. 64–65, and Haim Schwarzbaum, *Studies in Jewish and World Folklore* (Berlin: Walter de Grüyter, 1968), p. 92n.65.

In a labor camp.
—Why are you here?
—I went out into the main square and shouted, 'I'm hungry!' What about you?
—Well, with me it's the other way round.
—What do you mean?
— I too went into the main square, but I shouted, 'I'm fed up!'

Three men meet in a jail.
—What are you here for?
—Why, I went out and shouted, "Down with Vasile Luca." What are you here for?
—Oh, I shouted, "Long live Vasile Luca."
—What are you here for?
—Well, I am Vasile Luca.

This is an extremely popular joke. Lo Bello, 1966:23, claimed it was number one on the "Wit Parade" and that it was heard in Sofia, Bucharest, Budapest, Belgrade, East Berlin, Prague, and Warsaw. Reported versions bear this out with the variation centering upon the name of the individual. For Russian versions (about Karl Radek), see Wolfe, 1951:13, Winick, 1964:12. For other Russian versions, see Dor and

Federmann, 1964:215 (Comrade Popow), and Meyer, 1978:116 (Sacha Alexandrov). For other versions about Popov or Popow, see Kukin, 1962:[22]; Brandt, 1965:94–95; Benton and Loomes, 1976: 130; Hirche, 1977:134; and Kalina, 1980:28. For Polish versions about Gomulka, see Durocher, 1965:59–60; Drozdzynski, 1974:117; Paruit, 1978:58; and Melor, 1979:121. For an East German version about Khruschev, see Abrahams and Wukasch, 1967:9; for another East German text, see Hirche, 1964:241; for a Czech version about Richard Slánský, see Beckmann, 1969:16. For a German version about Hitler's old friend Röhm, see Larsen, 1980:45–46; for a German version about Hess, see Gamm, 1979[1963]:35. For a brief biographical sketch of Vasile Luca as well as other Romanian political figures mentioned in the jokes in this volume, see "Biographical Sketches of Leading Communists," in Stephen Fisher-Galati, ed., *Romania* (New York: Frederick A. Praeger, 1957), 344–50.

A discussion between two Russians in the days under Stalin.
—Have you ever been in jail?
—No.
—Never mind, you will be.
—Have you?
—Yes.
—Never mind, you will be again.

In a variant text, one finds the statement that the population of the Soviet Union can be divided into three parts: those who have been in prison; those who are in prison; and those who are waiting to go there. See Paruit, 1978:43.

In a labor camp in Stalin's time.
—How long are you in for?
—Fifteen years.
—What did you do?
—Me? Nothing.
—Oh, come on, everybody knows that for nothing one gets only ten years.

For another Romanian version, see anon., 1977:850. For Czech versions, see Beckmann, 1969:15; Swoboda, 1969:43; and Kalina,

1980:69. For other versions, see Brandt, 1965:95; Durocher, 1965:58–59; Kolasky, 1972:74; Drozdzynski, 1974:50; Benton and Loomes, 1976:130; Isnard, 1977:41; Meyer, 1978:114–15; Paruit, 1978:34; and Melor, 1979:132.

A question for Radio Erevan.
—Is it true that conditions in our labor camps are excellent?
—In principle, yes. Five years ago one of our listeners was not convinced of this, so he was sent there to investigate. He seems to have liked it so much that he hasn't returned yet.

For another version, see Kolasky, 1972:121.

At the Twentieth Congress of the Communist Party of the USSR while Khrushchev was denouncing Stalin's crimes, a voice was heard in the audience:
—Why didn't you, as old communists, open your mouths while Stalin was alive?
—Khruschev, startled, turned in the direction of the voice.
—Who asked that question? he asked.
Silence.
—I ask again the person who asked that question to stand up like a responsible communist.
Silence.
—You see, comrades? That's why.

For a Czech version, see Beckmann, 1969:38. For other versions, see Brandt, 1965:135–36; Kolasky, 1972:8–9; Drozdzynski, 1974:76; Benton and Loomes, 1976:93–94; and Dolgopolova, 1982:30.

The Bucharest circus is in trouble. People don't like the show. Fewer and fewer tickets are sold. Finally at a board meeting, Moritz comes up with an idea.
—All we have to do is announce that our show will conclude with a special number. Anyone who doesn't like it will be entitled to a tenfold refund. I can guarantee we'll sell the tickets one month in advance.
—Are you crazy? We'll go broke.
—Don't worry. I'd like to see who would dare ask for a refund if our

special number is an orchestra and choir performance of the "Interna-tional."

In one version, the circus director announces to a disgruntled circus audience that the final number will be the "orchestra of our heroic secret police playing for you the 'International'." See Melor, 1979:141–42. For other versions, see Kolasky, 1972:4, and Drozdzynski, 1974:46.

At school, a teacher discusses Homer's account of the Trojan war. He asks a student:
—Isaac, who took Troy?
—Comrade professor, it wasn't me.
The teacher is furious. He sends a note asking Isaac's father to come to school to see him. When the father arrives, the teacher tells him about his son's inept answer.
—Well, comrade teacher, says Mr. Rabinowitch, my son may not be a bright student, but he is not a liar. If he says he didn't take it, you may believe he really didn't.
The exasperated teacher complains to the principal.
—Well, says the principal, I know the family—honest working-class people. Maybe the kid really didn't take it.
Even more irritated, the teacher leaves for home, and on the way he runs into a friend who happens to be a K.G.B. officer. He tells him his annoyance over the answers of the Rabinowitches and the principal.
—You know, says the K.G.B. man, sometimes they do tell the truth.
The teacher goes home fuming at such ignorance and tries to forget the incident. A week later he again runs into his friend.
—By the way, says the K.G.B. officer, the Rabinowitches have con-fessed everything. They *took Troy.*

In an American version of this joke, the teacher asks a student who shot Abraham Lincoln. The student says he didn't do it. The boy's parent, summoned to school, insists if his boy said he didn't do it, he didn't do it. As the boy and his father leave the school, the father turns to his son and asks, "Tell me, son, did you do it?" See Larry Wilde, *The Official Dumb Parents Joke Book* (Los Angeles: Pinnacle Books, 1977), 1. It should be noted that the name Rabinowitch or some varia-tion thereof is one of the most common names given to Jews in east European jokes (cf. Meyer, 1978:23).

At an international conference on archeology, the discussion turns to a recently found mummy. There is as yet no evidence as to whose mummy it might be. The Russian delegation asks for permission to send the mummy to Moscow. Three days later, they make a full report.
—This is the mummy of . . . and full details follow.
The colleagues, amazed, ask how this knowledge was obtained.
—Oh, that's simple. We just lent it to the K.G.B. for three days, and the mummy confessed everything.

For another Romanian version, see Brunvand, 1973:187. For a version from Yugoslavia, see Lo Bello, 1966:26; for a Czech version, see Filip and Steiger, 1977:36. For other versions, see Kukin, 1962:[129]; Streit, 1964:28; Durocher, 1965:59; Mikes, 1971:145; Kolasky, 1972:74; Benton and Loomes, 1976:137; Hirche, 1977:188; Meyer, 1978:108; Paruit, 1978:31–32; Kalina, 1980:65; and Larsen, 1980:103.

Stalin has lost his pipe.
—This is sabotage! he exclaims.
He asks the secret police to find the culprit. Two hours later, he finds the pipe under his desk. He calls the secret police and asks them to forget about the investigation.
—But we can't stop now, the answer comes. We have arrested one hundred suspects, and fifty of them have already confessed.

The "missing pipe" joke is a standard one. For other versions, see Durocher, 1965:64–65; Kolasky, 1972:73; Draitser, 1978:15; Meyer, 1978:116; and Paruit, 1978:41–42. For a Czech version (told about Klement Gottwald), see Beckmann, 1969:14. In one version, it is Stalin's watch which is missing. See Hirche, 1964:282; Drozdzynski, 1974:62–63; and Kalina, 1980:67. In another, it is Stalin's briefcase containing secret papers; see Winick, 1964:18.

In another joke about confessions, a music student sits on the banks of the Danube reading the score of the Ninth Symphony. A police agent who had watched him for some time asked him what he was reading. "I'm reading notes." "What kind of notes?" "Beethoven notes!" "What are you saying? Do you think I'm so dumb that I can't see that you're reading a spy code? Come with me." The student spends many days in prison, but finally when he is brought to the chief of the secret police, he denies that it is a question of notes involving a spy report. The next day, the chief himself comes and shouts, "You idiot, there's no point in your further denials. Beethoven, whom we arrested yesterday, is sitting in the next cell, and he says that he never gave you any notes." See Hirche, 1964:299; Hirche, 1977:170; and Kalina, 1980:73. In another version, the final lines from the chief interrogator are: "We've had enough of your lies! You might just as well tell us everything—your friend Tchaikovsky has already confessed." See Benton and Loomes, 1976:122–23.

—What's the difference between a theoretical physicist and K.G.B. agent?

—A theoretical physicist says, give me any physical facts and I will find a theory. A K.G.B. man says, give me any man and I will find a charge.

For another version, see Kolasky, 1972:74.

A man is in his garden when three men appear.

—We've been informed that you have hidden gold coins in your garden.

—That's a lie. I don't own any coins.

—Who are you trying to fool? Get out of the way.

Two hours later, the policemen leave emptyhanded. The man's wife emerges from the house.

—Wasn't I right to send the K.G.B. that little note? When would you have found the time to dig the garden by yourself?

For a variant, see Paruit, 1978:38.

An American tourist strolling through Moscow by night sees a black truck rushing by. With a sudden jolt a big sack falls out of it. To the American's amazement, the sack is moving as if something alive were in it. He opens the sack, and who should pop out of it but his old friend Sammy.

—Sammy, what's the matter with you? Why were you in that sack?

—I was being taken from one prison to another for interrogation by the K.G.B. But what are you doing in Moscow? Aren't you an American citizen now?

—Sure I am. I was touring Europe and came as far as Moscow. Say, Sammy, do you remember the old times when we toiled and starved together at Auschwitz?
—Yeah, those were the days!

This very bitter joke refers to the tragic fact that although nobody could imagine anything worse than the Nazi death camps, the refinement in cruelty of K.G.B. interrogations has never been equalled—even by the Gestapo. For other versions of the joke, see Paruit, 1978:38–39; and Kalina, 1980:64–65. For an early study of gallows humor, see Antonin J. Obrdlik, "'Gallows Humor'—A Sociological Phenomenon," *American Journal of Sociology* 47 (1942): 709–16. For a startling account of jokes about Auschwitz told by Germans, see Alan Dundes and Thomas Hauschild, "Auschwitz Jokes," *Western Folklore* 42 (1983): 249–60.

Question for Radio Erevan.
—Yesterday I had an argument with a colleague over who the most worthy member of our leadership is. I said Brezhnev. Was I right?
—Radio Erevan apologizes for a break in transmission due to a sudden storm.

It is dangerous to criticize leaders in public. Another Radio Erevan text suggests this. "Dear Radio Erevan. I don't know what's the matter with me. I don't love the Party any more. I feel nothing at all for Comrade Brezhnev or any of the other leaders of the Party. What should I do?" Radio Erevan's answer, "Please send us your name and address." See Benton and Loomes, 1976:144. For another version, see Schiff, 1969:69.

—Why has the radio reception recently been so bad?
—Because it is now transmitting from Magadan [in Siberia].

For other versions, see Durocher, 1965:73; Paruit, 1978:198–99; and Larsen, 1980:87. Apparently, wayward radio stations, like troublesome individuals, can be shipped off to Siberia. The exile of dissidents to Siberia continues to be a popular theme in east European political humor. For example, a Czech text goes as follows: "Seeking to purchase Siberia, the United States made an initial bid of a fantastic sum of money. The Soviet leaders reluctantly refused. The offer, they said, was most attractive, but such a deal would entail the loss of all their intellectuals." See "Current Humor in Czechoslovakia," *East Europe,* 18, nos. 11–12 (November–December, 1969): 52. In a Czech variant, the question "What would happen if the Americans dropped an atomic bomb on Siberia?" is answered with "The intellectuals of the Soviet Union would lose the roof over their heads." See Kalina, 1980:183.

The Six Commandments of a writer in a communist country:
1. *Don't think.*
2. *If you do think, don't talk.*
3. *If you do talk, don't write it down.*
4. *If you do write it, don't publish it.*
5. *If you do publish it, don't sign it.*
6. *If you do sign it, write a denial.*

For other versions, see Dallin, 1949:15; anon., 1977:850; Meyer, 1978:90; Paruit, 1978:83–84; and Kalina, 1980:36.

3
The Ministry of Truth

Question:
—Is it true that the composer Khachaturian has won a car at a lottery?
Answer:
—In principle, yes, but there are some small corrections to be made. It's not Khachaturian, but Shostakovich; it's not a car, but a motorcycle; he didn't win it, but he lost it; and it wasn't at the lottery, but at stud poker.

Although apparently apolitical, this joke has political overtones. It alludes to the step-by-step distortion of facts by the official propaganda which results in totally falsified accounts of events and situations. In another version of the joke, Radio Erevan replies that the report that Shostakovich was given a blue automobile for his accomplishments is true, but it wasn't a car, it was a bicycle; it wasn't blue, it was green; and he wasn't offered it, he stole it. See Paruit, 1978:195–96; cf. 197–98. For other versions, see Schiff, 1969:40; Hirche, 1977:142–43; Draitser, 1978:19; and Kalina, 1980:169.

A question is sent to Radio Erevan.
—Is it true that the poet Maiakovski committed suicide?
—Yes, it is true that Maiakovski committed suicide, and we even have recorded his very last words: "Don't shoot, comrades!"

This joke was also collected by folklorist Jan Brunvand who carried out fieldwork in Romania. Brunvand used the joke's punch line as the title of his article "Don't Shoot, Comrades: A Survey of the Submerged Folklore of Eastern Europe," *North Carolina Folklore Journal* 21

(1973): 181–88. For other versions, see Drozdzynski, 1974:69; Meyer, 1978:120; Paruit, 1978:27–28; Melor, 1979:142; and Kalina, 1980:66.

—*Have you heard that they have arrested the entire staff of the Central Bookstore?*
—*No, why?*
—*Because they have put three books on display in the shop window in the following order:* We Want to Live, Far from Moscow, In the Shadow of the Skyscrapers.

One of the most dangerous traits of communist rule is the government leaders' attempt to totally control the people's minds. Not only are many of the world's greatest literary works banned, or worse, their content distorted by error or omission, but ideological writings (including, of course, books with anti-American content) are required reading. More than in any other area, the famous quip "everything that is not forbidden is compulsory" applies. Under Stalin, certain "masterpieces of Soviet thought" were obligatory reading. Of course, such a dictum could never be thoroughly enforced, but nevertheless these writings at least had to be translated into the native languages of all eastern European countries with pressure exerted on citizens to buy these translations.

In an early Czech version of the above joke, there are four titles: *We Want to Live; Far from Moscow; In the Shadows of Skyscrapers; Under a Foreign Flag.* See "Title Role," *News from Behind the Iron Curtain,* 1, no. 2 (February, 1952): 43. For a later Czech text, see Beckmann, 1969:22.

After his death, a Romanian knocks at the gates of heaven. St. Peter appears and tells him he is not on his list so he'd better try at the competitor's gate.

As soon as he reaches hell, the gates are opened for him, and two devils invite him kindly to take a place at a banquet table. The hall is beautiful, the table setting dazzling, the food and drink delicious. Beautiful girls surround him, sweet music is played in the background. After a while, he finds hell rather boring, but unlike what he had expected, pleasant enough. All of a sudden, a voice announces through a loudspeaker that his was only an apparent death and that he must therefore return to earth.

He lives another ten years and then dies for good. This time he doesn't even attempt to go to heaven, which is unknown to him, but he goes right to hell. But as soon as he arrives, two devils grab him and throw him into boiling tar. He complains and asks for an explanation, but to no avail. Finally the department head arrives and asks what all the fuss is about.

—There must be a mistake. I've been here on another occasion, and it looked quite different.

—Oh, that! That was the hell for tourists.

For another Romanian version, see Beckmann, 1969:115. For other versions, see "Only Joking," *News from Behind the Iron Curtain,* 2, no. 4 (April, 1953): 55; Winick, 1964:20; Kolasky, 1972:7; Drozd-zynski, 1974:61; Isnard, 1977:64; Paruit, 1978:167–68; and Kalina, 1980:176. For a Nazi German version, see Gamm, 1979[1963]:69.

There is no doubt that the Soviet Union as well as all communist countries put on special displays for tourists. Tourists in the Soviet Union, for example, are normally handled by Intourist and are not free to go wherever they wish whenever they wish. Tourists who see only what they are shown may get a misleading picture of the country. The difference between appearance and reality is obviously the subject of the above joke about hell for tourists, but it is also beautifully de-lineated in a joke in which a foreigner asks a Moscow friend about the status of the concept of peaceful coexistence in the Soviet Union. The Russian asks the questioner to follow him and tells him that he will understand. The Russian leads him to the zoo and stops in front of a cage which is shared by a bear and a lamb. "Look there!" the West-erner agrees that it is splendid example of peaceful coexistence. As they leave the zoo, they come upon a caretaker who grumbles, "Yes, but that costs us a lot." "Why is that?" "Because we have to change the lamb three times a day." See Paruit, 1978:152–53; and Kalina, 1980:249. An earlier version had a wolf and a lamb with the lamb changed daily. See Kukin, 1962:[144]. For other versions of the wolf and the lamb, see Hirche, 1964:290; Brandt, 1965:147; and Benton and Loomes, 1976:151–52. It is not entirely clear whether the fable is in-tended to evoke the famous lines of Isaiah (11:6) which indicate that one sign of the millennium will be when "The wolf also shall dwell with the lamb."

A man dies and his soul is directed to hell. To his amazement, he sees that life there appears to be very pleasant. Everyone is seated at a table, a glass of wine in his hand, and a pretty girl in his lap. Some

couples are lying on couches in a dark corner of the room. Music is
heard in the background.
  —*Is this hell? Am I not at the wrong address? he asks.*
  —*Not at all, says a devil. Things here aren't what they seem.*
  —*What do you mean? What about those pretty girls?*
  —*It's an illusion. They are girls only from the waist up.*
  —*And the wine?*
It looks like wine, it even smells like wine, but as soon as you take it
into your mouth it turns into gall.
  —*And the couches? Aren't they real?*
They're all lined with sharp nails.
But the music!
  —*You call that music? That's by Mateescu.*

Not only literature but the arts too are under party control. During
the Stalinist years especially, the only artistic works accepted were
those dedicated to the party, its leaders, and it glorious achievements.
This kind of art is called in Newspeak "socialist realism."

To understand the above joke, one needs to know that a mediocre
composer (who, incidentally, did actually believe in communism) has
reached the highest position in the musical life of Bucharest because of
his compositions glorifying the party. All true music lovers chafed at
the rubbish they were obliged to hear in concert halls, intermingled
with real music. As usual, such individuals let off steam in jokes making fun of this composer whom we have given the name Mateescu. For
other versions of this joke, see Beckmann, 1969:26, and Paruit,
1978:171.

The terrible Mongol leader Genghis Khan was known to be hunch-
backed and to have a cast on one eye. Nevertheless, he once asked a
famous artist to paint his portrait. The painter completed an excellent
portrait, but it was all too realistic, showing all the physical defects of
the mighty emperor. As expected, Genghis Khan ordered the painter's
head cut off.
  The next painter tried to be smart, and his portrait showed a hand-
some man having hardly any resemblance to its model. He too had his
head cut off because Genghis Khan declared he was not going to be
made a fool of.
  The third painter tried a new approach. His portrait showed Genghis
Khan riding a horse, his face turned to one side so that only the good
eye could be seen, his sword raised in a gesture that made his back

look straighter. Genghis Khan showered gifts upon him, and he lived happily ever after.

. . . And this painter was the man who laid the foundations of socialist realism in art.

For other versions of this joke, see Dor and Federmann, 1964:216–17; Brandt, 1965:123–24; Drozdzynski, 1974:73; Paruit, 1978:170; Melor, 1979:86; and Kalina, 1980:180–81. There are many jokes about socialist realism. For example, what is the difference between a realist, impressionist, and socialist realist painter? A realist painter paints what he sees, an impressionist painter paints what he feels, and a socialist realist painter paints what he hears (or in some versions "what he is told"). See Durocher, 1965:103; Kolasky, 1972:141; anon., 1977:790; and Kalina, 1980:180.

Besides the indoctrination through "trade union" meetings, everyone is forced to take specific indoctrination courses, from the first school year up to the age of retirement.

Moshe was assigned to a course on dialectics. Not knowing what it was all about, he went to see his rabbi.

—Rabbi, what is dialectics?

—Oh, it's very simple. Suppose two chimney sweeps get out of a chimney and one of them is dirty, the other one is clean. Which one takes a bath?

—The dirty one, of course.

—Wrong. The dirty one looks at his companion, sees that he is clean, and thinks that he too is clean. The clean one looks at his companion, and concluding he is dirty, he goes to take a bath.

—So this is dialectics?

—No, wait. Two chimney sweeps get out of a chimney, one dirty and one clean. Which one takes a bath?

—You just proved that it's the clean one.

—Wrong again. They both look at their hands, and the dirty one goes to take a bath. Let's try again. Two chimney sweeps . . .

—Stop, rabbi, I begin to get confused.

—Be patient, if you want to understand. Now two chimney sweeps get out of a chimney, one dirty and one clean. One of them is dirty, the other one is clean. Which of them takes a bath?

—Isn't it the dirty one?

—No. Both of them. The dirty one looks at his hands, while the clean

one looks at his companion, and he supposes he is just as dirty. Once more. Two chimney sweeps get . . .

—Useless, rabbi, whatever I say will be wrong. You seem to twist things so as to make out of them whatever suits you a given moment.

—Now you finally understand the essence of dialectics. And since you do, let me give you a problem. Two chimney sweeps get out of a chimney, one dirty and one clean. Which one takes a bath?

—Which one suits you now?

—Neither. Who the hell has ever seen a chimney sweep getting out of a chimney clean?

This is an extremely popular tale, often told in the West as a parody of Talmudic reasoning. For a version said to date from 1938, see Benton and Loomes, 1976:150. For an East German text, see Brandt, 1965:117–18. For Polish versions, see "Definitive Dialectics," *News from Behind the Iron Curtain,* 1, no. 7 (July, 1952): 48, and Dor and Federmann, 1964:252–53; for a Hungarian version, see "The Lesson," *East Europe,* 9, no. 11 (November, 1960): 7; for Czech versions, see Beckmann, 1969:68–69; Swoboda, 1969:54–56; and Kalina, 1980:80. For other versions, see Durocher, 1965:153–64; Jacobi, 1965:95; and Hirche, 1977:136–37.

Question:
—What features has the Soviet society retained from the various stages in the historical development of human societies?
Answer:
—From primitive society, a philosophy of life; from antiquity, slavery; from feudalism, the hierarchy; from capitalism, exploitation, and from socialism, the name.

For a Polish version, "Communism is a system that takes from the Stone Age its technical level, from slavery its social relations, from feudalism its hierarchy, from capitalism its exploitation, and from socialism its name," see Langnas, 1963:20. For a Hungarian version, see Jacobi, 1965:13; for East German versions, see Brandt, 1965:79; Drozdzynski, 1974:180; and Larsen, 1980:94. For other versions, see Hirche, 1964:228; Anon., 1971:10; Benton and Loomes, 1976:141; Melor, 1979:223; and Kalina, 1980:78, 242.

Popescu meets a friend at the factory canteen.
—Why are you eating here? Weren't you recently married?
—Yes, but my wife is very young and doesn't know how to cook.
—Why don't you send her to an evening course in cooking?
Six weeks later, the two friends meet again.
—How come you still eat here? Hasn't your wife taken a cooking course?
—She still attends it, but up until now they only managed to get as far as the Great Socialist October Revolution.

For other versions, see Brandt, 1965:118–19; Swoboda, 1969:11–12; Benton and Loomes, 1976:122; Kalina, 1980:87; and Larsen, 1980:95. The concerted effort to politicize all types of education is a common subject for jokes. A joke from Poland which circulated in the Slavic Department at the University of California, Berkeley, in 1970, further illustrates this point. A teacher questions his class. "Tell me, what is fluffy, red, has small, black eyes, and a big beautiful tail?" "I don't know," answers one student. "What do you mean you don't know? Think again . . . a little, small, fluffy thing with a beautiful tail." "If my mother had asked me, I would have answered that it was a squirrel. Since you are asking, it must be Lenin."

In 1951, two Romanians, heroes of socialist work, are each awarded a two-week trip to the Soviet Union. When the trip is over, only one of them comes back. His colleagues assail him with questions.
—How are living conditions in the Soviet Union?
—Excellent, I couldn't believe my eyes.
—How is the housing? How is the food situation?
—Excellent, I couldn't believe my eyes.
—What about the working conditions?
—Wonderful, I couldn't believe my eyes.
—But where is your friend Mitica?
—He is still in Siberia. It seems he *could believe his eyes.*

For another version, see Meyer, 1978:112.

Stalin chats with Radek, the editor in chief of Pravda *(a witty intellectual of the old communist guard which was gradually eradicated by Stalin).*

—What a fine sight those new high rises must be, which according to Pravda *are springing up on the shores of the Moscow River.*

—But comrade Stalin, I strolled along those shores this morning, and I didn't see any new buildings there.

—Comrade Radek, if you'd stroll less and read Pravda *more, you'd be better informed about the accomplishments of our socialist state.*

For a Russian version, see Dallin, 1949:15. For a Czech version, see "Socialist Realism," *News from Behind the Iron Curtain,* 1, no. 11 (November, 1952): 53–54. For other versions, see Kukin, 1962:[72]; Dor and Federmann, 1964:234–35; Kolasky, 1972:86; Isnard, 1977:75; Melor, 1979:99–100; and Kalina, 1980:168.

The discrepancy between what one is told and what one can empirically observe is a favorite joke topic. For example, a Hungarian walked into a Budapest hospital and asked for the eye and ear section. The nurse told him the sections were separate; there was one for eyes and one for ears. "Oh, but I must go to both," exclaimed the Hungarian. "I don't know what has happened to me during the last few years. I don't see what I hear." See "Difficult to Diagnose," *News from Behind the Iron Curtain,* 1, no. 5 (May, 1952): 39. For other versions, see Winick, 1964:38, and Beckmann, 1969:104.

Another joke which plays upon the disparity between propaganda and reality tells of an individual complaining that although the radio announces there is plenty of food, his refrigerator is always empty. He is advised to plug his refrigerator directly into his radio. For representative versions, see Winick, 1964:37; Hirche, 1964:287; Kolasky, 1972:91; Benton and Loomes, 1976:143; Meyer, 1978:68; Paruit, 1978:159; and Melor, 1979:99, 218.

One of the most apt commentaries on radio reporting is the joke which claims there are three types of news on Czech radio: the true, for example, the weather conditions of the day; the possible, for example, weather forecasts; and the false, which is everything else. See Melor, 1979:100.

Radek is present at a general party meeting at which all the Soviet republics are represented. An Uzbek delegate comes to the rostrum. Comrade Radek translates into Russian. A Ukrainian delegate comes to the rostrum. Comrade Radek translates. An Armenian delegate comes to the rostrum. Comrade Radek translates. A guest from the German Communist party, sitting next to Radek, happens to understand Armenian. He objects:

—But comrade Radek, this man never said what you translated.
—Never mind, this is what he should have said.

For other versions of this joke, see Kukin, 1962:[114]; Dor and
Federmann, 1964:325–26; Drozdzynski, 1974:28–29; and Melor,
1979:56. Sometimes, translators are more honest. A Russian scientist
is delivering a lecture in Peking. A Chinese interpreter was assigned to
translate the talk. When the Russian completed the first of three long
parts of his lecture, the Chinese interpreter said just one word: "Ping."
The audience applauded loudly. Though puzzled by the brevity of the
translation, the Russian went on. After the second part was finished,
the Chinese interpreter said: "Ping hong!" The listeners cheered. When
the last part of the lecture was over, the interpreter said, "Ping hong
chung." The reaction shook the rafters. As the lecturer thanked the
interpreter, he commended him an the apparent success of his translation but wondered about its extreme brevity. The Chinese explained:
"My first 'ping' meant 'nonsense,' my 'ping hong' was 'more nonsense,' and my final 'ping hong chung' indicated 'end of nonsense.' See
Parry, 1966:41. For other versions, see Lewis, 1956:12; Brandt,
1965:214, and Durocher, 1965:131–32. A similar device is employed in
a joke in which President Nixon sends Secretary of State Henry Kissinger on a goodwill tour to Africa. In one town, Kissinger addresses a
huge meeting. "We will build you a new technical college." "Bella-
bella," his audience shouted. "And we will build you a large modern
reservoir." "Bella-bella, bella-bella." Pleased with his reception, Kissinger asked if he could walk about and meet the people. "Certainly," he
was told, "But we should warn you that the cattle wander all over the
town. Be careful you don't step in the bella-bella." See Benton and
Loomes, 1976:50–51.

---

*Peaceful coexistence. A Soviet and an American were arguing over
which of their cars was the faster and finally decided to settle the
matter by a race. The American car proved to be faster. Next day, the
event was reported in* Pravda *as follows: At an international rally, the
Soviet car placed second. The American car finished next to last.*

For other versions, see Kukin, 1962:[3]; Dor and Federmann,
1964:240; Winick, 1964:49; Brandt, 1965:142, Beckmann, 1969:44;
Schiff, 1969:39; Swoboda, 1969:17–18; Drozdzynski, 1974:81–82;
Benton and Loomes, 1976:119; Melor, 1979:97–98; and Dolgopolova,
1982:28–29.

In Moscow a little boy asks his father:
—*Daddy, what is anti-Soviet propaganda?*
—*Well, it's like this. Suppose an American diver dives six thousand feet into the Atlantic. At the same time, a Russian diver dives ten thousand feet into the Black Sea. What do you make of it?*
—*That it's a lie. The Black Sea is only eight thousand feet at its deepest.*
—*You see? That's anti-Soviet propaganda.*

For other versions, see Isnard, 1977:78 and Melor, 1979:105.

During a state visit to the Soviet Union, Gheorghiu-Dej (then party and state boss) once asked Khrushchev:
—*How do you manage to get so many people to enroll for voluntary labor? What kind of coercion do you use?*
—*We never use any coercion in the Soviet Union. We manage to persuade people to do it of their own free will.*
—*We've tried that, too, but with very poor results.*
—*That's because you don't know how to go about it. Look, take as an example this cat. Do you think I can talk her into licking mustard?*
—*Certainly not.*
—*I can, however, persuade her to do it of her own free will. Look.*
Khrushchev took the cat in his arms, and with a swift, deft movement, smeared it with mustard under the tail.
—*You see, now he licks the mustard uncompelled.*

For other versions, see Kukin, 1962:[109], and Kalina, 1980:123. For an earlier German version, see Hans Förster, "Erzählungen aus den Vierlanden, Schaumburg-Lippe, Westfalen und Hamburg," *Anthropophyteia Jahrbücher* 9 (1912): 410–11.

Question for Radio Erevan.
—*Is it true that Russian U-boats hold the record for extended submersion?*
—*In principle, yes. Two of them have been on the bottom since 1957.*

For another version, see Schiff, 1969:116.

There is a dwarf in New York who lives on the 150th floor of a building, but he can reach only the fiftieth button in the elevator. Some-

one else must push the top button for him. In the Soviet Union, there is also a dwarf who lives on the 150th floor, but he pushes the top button. Why? Because Soviet dwarfs are the greatest dwarfs in the world!

A Polish version of this joke takes the form of a question: What is the difference between Soviet dwarfs and American dwarfs? The Soviet are bigger. See Langnas, 1963:20. For other versions of this form, see Hirche, 1964:295; Brandt, 1965:27, 152; Durocher, 1965:69; Schiff, 1975:64; and Isnard, 1977:30. For additional versions of the joke in the format reported here, see Beckmann, 1969:75; Schiff, 1969:34; Drozdzynski, 1974:89; and Paruit, 1978:148. Other versions simply use the dwarf case as "proof" of the superiority of the Soviet Union over the United States. A Russian text boasts that "A Soviet dwarf is two centimetres taller than a capitalist dwarf," (Dolgopolova, 1982:83) while a Czech text reports on a Russian plan to overtake the United States by developing the greatest dwarfs and the fastest clocks in the world (Kalina, 1980:142).

At an international conference on entomology, there is a section dealing with lice. Some of the papers submitted concern scientific aspects of lice physiology. Most papers, however, are devoted to recent developments in chemistry which had helped to eradicate this pest. The Soviet Union is represented at the conference. The paper submitted by its scientists is entitled: "The Happy Life of Lice in the Soviet Union."

According to another Romanian version, the title of the paper is: "The Soviet Lice, the Happiest Lice in the World." In a variant, it is the Russian elephants who are the happiest elephants in the world. See Paruit, 1978:149.

A question for Radio Erevan.
  —Can bedbugs make a revolution?
  —In principle, yes, for in their veins there flows the blood of peasants and workers.

The answer to the question plays upon a frequently used slogan intended to emphasize the class character of the proletarian revolution. For other versions of the joke, see Schiff, 1969:34; Hirche, 1977:139; and Kalina, 1980:230.

There is an international conference on elephants.
The British scientists submit a paper entitled, "The Elephant and the British Empire."
The Germans send in a twelve volume set of books entitled, "An Introduction to the Study of the Elephant."
The French scholars submit a paper, "L'amour chez les elephants."
The Russians submit two papers: "Marx, Engels, Lenin, and Stalin on Elephants" and "The Happy Life of Elephants in the Soviet Union."
The Romanians submit a paper entitled, "The Soviet Elephant, the Most Advanced Elephant in the World."

For other versions, see Brandt, 1965:145; Beckmann, 1969:77; Benton and Loomes, 1976:120–21; Isnard, 1977:110. For an American version, see Alan Dundes, "Slurs International: Folk Comparisons of Ethnicity and National Character," *Southern Folklore Quarterly* 39 (1975): 32–33.

There are many jokes ridiculing the way in which east European politicians ape Moscow's actions and words. One of the classics has Ulbricht—or some similar figure—walking down the street with an umbrella on a day when the sun is shining brightly. When asked to account for his strange behavior, he explains that it is raining in Moscow. For representative texts, see Kukin, 1962:[146]; Brandt, 1965:225; Lo Bello, 1966:25; Beckmann, 1969:113; Swoboda, 1969:15; Drozdynski, 1974:174; Isnard, 1977:23; and Kalina, 1980:34. In a variant, a Bulgarian official arrives at the ministry one beautiful spring morning muffled in a thick shepherd's overcoat. When his colleagues ask him if he is ill, he replies, no but the radio announced that it had snowed in Leningrad. See Paruit, 1978:137. For an East German version in which Ulbricht wears a coat because it's snowing in Moscow, see Durocher, 1965:156, and Benton and Loomes, 1976:105.

The subservient nature of eastern European governments and peoples to the Soviet Union is a popular subject in jokes. A common one, for example, is the strange nature of the particular type of telephone used in these countries for direct communication with Moscow. The model consists of a receiver only. For representative texts, see Hirche, 1964:221; Brandt, 1965:225; Jacobi, 1965:40; Lo Bello, 1966:25; Swoboda, 1969:25; Kolasky, 1972:30; Benton and Loomes, 1976:105; and Paruit, 1978:140. The plight is beautifully described in a Hungarian joke the second author collected in Budapest in August 1979: An official in an eastern country is talking on the telephone to Moscow. His secretary in the adjacent office hears one end of the conversation: Da, Da, Da, Da, Niet, Da, Da, Da. At the end of the conversation, the secretary rushes into the official's office with great concern saying, "I couldn't help but overhear. What could Moscow possibly have said to you to make you say 'Niet.'" "Oh, don't worry," explained the official, "They just asked me if I got tired of saying 'yes' all the time." For a Czech variant in which the "no" is in response to Moscow's question "Is it raining in Prague?" see Kalina, 1980:34 cf. Swoboda, 1969:21. An interesting inversion of this joke occurs in texts emphasizing the Russian end of the conversation: During the Berlin blockade, a meeting of the Politbureau was held at the Kremlin. Suddenly the telephone rings. Molotov is called to the phone. He listens and then responds, "—Niet,—Niet,—Niet,—Niet, niet, niet.—Niet." After an instant of silence, Molotov says, "Da." Molotov hangs up. "Why did you say 'yes'?" his comrades ask in chorus. "They asked me if I have answered everything 'niet'." See Durocher, 1965:153.

—What would you rather be in Romania? You can be head of a ministry department. You then would have 6,000 lei per month, a chauffeur-driven car, a pretty blonde secretary, huge fringe benefits including access to some of the big wigs' special stores and rest houses, frequent paid trips abroad. It's not too bad to be the director of a big plant either. Less responsibility, 4,500 lei per month. You can get a new imported car without being on the waiting list; you get free service at the plant's workshops, large fringe benefits.

But best of all is to be a capita. You then have so many tons of steel per year, so many tons of . . .

The reference to a waiting list for car purchase may not be clear to Western readers. Normally in order to buy a car, one must pay in full and then wait six months for the Romanian produced Dacia or up to three years for an imported car. For another version of the joke, see Paruit, 1978:93.

At a school in the Soviet Union during an indoctrination course, the instructor gives a talk extolling the wonderful life of Soviet children. They are all well dressed, he says, they have modern schools where they get the best education, they can afford all the toys they dream of, they have excellent facilities for sports available in the Soviet Union to every single child, and they have marvelous summer camps.

After the lecture, an informal discussion takes place, and the children are asked what they would like to be when they grow up. One would like to become an engineer, another one an astronaut, a third one an athlete. Only little Ivan keeps quiet, so the instructor asks him to speak.

—What I wish most, says Ivan, is to become . . . a Soviet child.

For a version set in Bulgaria, see anon. 1977:671. For another version, see Kalina, 1980:42.

In order to disprove the Western world's criticism regarding the lack of freedom of the Romanian workers, Ceausescu decides to stage a strike and to invite foreign reporters to see it. A trade union meeting is called at a factory, and the trade union leader, well instructed, tries to raise the workers' anger:

—Comrades, from now on we are going to work twelve hours daily with the exception of Sundays when we will work only eight hours, until we fulfill our plan.

All the workers, well trained by so many years of Communist rule, applaud enthusiastically, and the sixty-eight hour week is accepted.

Next week, another trade union meeting.

—Comrades, I am sorry to report that among us there still are some comrades who haven't understood the high objectives of our socialist endeavor. I'm determined to curb this attitude. From now on, whoever slows down the rhythm of production by not showing up on Sundays will have his monthly salary cut by half.

The workers approve, without objection.

At his wit's end, the leader announces:

—And no leave of absence will be granted, for whatever reason. From now on, all absentees will be hanged.

Somebody raises his hand. The leader asks, full of hope:

—What is it, comrade Popescu? Any objection?

—Oh no, I only want to know, should we bring our own rope, or will the factory provide it?

For another Romanian version, see Meyer, 1978:109–10. For a version set in Bulgaria, see Paruit, 1978:82–83.

It is October 1950. An American delegation is expected in Bucharest. Unfortunately, this is the time when the potato ration for the coming winter is on sale, and huge lines are forming at all markets. The leaders, not knowing how to cope with this situation which gives the lie to the image of prosperity they so desperately are trying to convey, seek the advice of a well-known economist whose recently published book The Happy Life under Socialism *has won him a high position in the Party.*

—Look, says the economist, all you have to do is to replace the signs of the vegetable shops by others which read: Savings. The Americans will think people have so much money that they're forming lines to deposit it in savings accounts.

The advice is followed; the impression created is the one desired. The Party wants to show its gratitude.

—You have rendered a great service to the country. What would you like as a reward?

—An emigration visa, please.

For East German variants, see Dor and Federmann, 1964:154; Benton and Loomes, 1976:106. In another version set in Romania, it is a butcher who saves the day by proposing that a "Bank" sign replace "Butcher Shop." A grateful Ceausescu offers him the post of finance minister. The butcher refuses. "What would you like? I will grant you any wish." "That no one will hereafter ask me where I have gotten my meat" (Kalina, 1980:137).

In 1968 President Nixon visited Romania. As he was scheduled to visit a factory, some workers have been well instructed on how to describe their lives and how to answer any questions that the United States president might ask them. However, to make absolutely sure that no unpleasant blunder could happen, a microphone and a buzzer were installed at each of their lathes. If an answer was not satisfactory, a short buzz would discreetly signal that some improvement of the statement was to be made.

Nixon arrived and started a conversation.

—Are you satisfied with your working conditions?

—Very satisfied, Mr. President.

—How many persons do you support on your salary?

—I have four children, Mr. President, and my wife is a worker too.

—How much do you make together?

—Two thousand per month, Mr. President.

Buzzer.

—. . . per person, Mr. President.

—How large is your apartment?

—Two rooms, Mr. President.
Buzzer.
—. . . per person, Mr. President.
—Great. And what hobby do you have?
No reply. Apparently the worker doesn't know what to say.
—Five and a half inches, Mr. President.
—Buzzer.
—. . . at rest, Mr. President.

4
In Short Supply

—What is one hundred meters long and eats cabbage?
—The line in front of a meat market.

For a Polish version, see Langnas, 1963:20. The question differs
slightly in another Polish text: "What's fifty meters long and eats
potatoes?" but the answer is the same: "A queue waiting to buy meat."
See "Jokes Current in East Europe," *East Europe,* 17, no. 3 (March,
1968):48; and Larsen, 1980:90. For another Romanian version, see
Brunvand, 1973:183. For other versions, see Hirche, 1964:256;
Durocher, 1965:72; Drozdzynski, 1974:96; Isnard, 1977:16; Melor,
1979:35; Kalina, 1980:161; and Davies, 1981:153.

A man comes home and finds his wife in bed with another man.
—You bitch, he exclaims, this is no time to make love when they have
meat at the corner market and the line is already forming!

For East German versions in which the line forming is for oranges,
see Hirche, 1964:256, and Adolph Schalk, *The Germans* (Englewood
Cliffs, N.J.: Prentice-Hall, 1971), 65. For a Russian version (with the
line for oranges), see Draitser, 1978:35. For other versions (with the
line for lemons), see Winick, 1964:55; Brandt, 1965:61; and Larsen,
1980:95.

An East German visits a friend in Moscow. A little girl answers the
door. The East German asks her:
—Where is your father?
—He is not home.

—When will he be at home?
—At eight hours, forty minutes and twenty-three seconds.
—Where is he?
—He is going around the world thirty-three and a half times.
—What about your mother? Is she at home?
—No, she isn't.
—When is she expected?
—I don't have any idea.
—How come you know the hour, minute, and second when your father will return, but you have no idea when your mother will return? Where is she?
—She is at the market in the line for meat.

For Russian versions of the cosmonaut's wife waiting for meat, see Drozdzynski, 1974:106, and Melor, 1979:38. In other Russian versions, the commodity in short supply varies. For potatoes, see Paruit, 1978:107–8; for flour, see Kalina, 1980:146; for milk, see Hirche, 1964:302, and Brandt, 1965:158; for shoes, see Dor and Federmann, 1964:239–40; and Benton and Loomes, 1976:102. For a version in which the object is unspecified, see Winick, 1964:33.

Two Jews, one from Romania and one from the Soviet Union, are talking about great men in their countries.
—Our rabbi in Botosani is terrific. I remember one Yom Kippur Eve. He said once Kol Nidre! and all the congregation fasted for twenty-four hours.
—That's nothing, said the other, we in the Soviet Union have Stalin. He once said Kolkhoz [Soviet collective farms], and all the population has been fasting ever since.

—Did you hear the joke about the living-space agent who isn't on the take?
—No.
—Of course not. There is no such thing.

In order to understand this joke, one must know that because of the acute housing shortage in eastern Europe, space and rent for such space are regulated by law. The agency created in Romania for this purpose was called colloquially "the living space agency." The agency was responsible for the assignment of rooms or apartments. Until the

1960s, practically no new houses were constructed by the government, and of course no private construction was permitted. The assigned "living space" was obtained by dividing or subdividing larger apartments among several families. So acute was the housing shortage that people were willing to go to any length in order to obtain the legal living space (ten square yards per person) even if this meant they had to pay disproportionate bribes to the agents who decided who would get which space in which housing unit. Such bribes were paid regardless of the huge financial burden this would entail for families concerned. Obviously the agents took full advantage of this situation. Except for individuals with special political status, bribery was the only way of obtaining one's legal space. During the 1960s, a housing project was initiated by the government which partially eased the shortage and dramatically lowered bribe rates since a new law legalized ownership of a standard apartment. The joke above had wide circulation in Bucharest during the 1950s.

A student's complaint:
—When you have a girl, you don't have a room. When you have a room, you don't have a girl. And when you have both girl and room, you have a party meeting.

A Polish version is similar: "What is the difference between comedy, tragedy, and Socialist realism? Comedy was before the war when you had a girl and couldn't afford to take her out. Tragedy was during the war when you couldn't find a girl and there was no place to take her. Socialist realism is now when you have a girl and you can take her out, but you never have time because you always have to go to a party meeting." See Lewis, 1956:12. In a more recent version, tragedy is when you have a girl but no room; comedy is when you have a room and no girl, and Socialist realism is when you have both a room and a girl, but must go to be trained. See Hirche, 1977:141. For an East German text, see Brandt, 1965:124. For a version from Yugoslavia, see Jacobi, 1965:141. For a Russian version, see Winick, 1964:9.

An old lady enters a food store in Bucharest and asks for a dozen eggs. The vendor tells her:
—You're in the wrong store, granny. Here we haven't got any meat. It's next door that they haven't got any eggs.

For another version (in which the vendor responding to a request for meat explains that this is the store where cheese isn't found. The store where there's no meat is across the street), see Paruit, 1978:107. In a variant, the response is "Here we have no milk. No meat is across the way," Kalina, 1980:165. For a version in which the inquiring customer is directed: "Over there is the department where they haven't got any caviar," see Larsen, 1980:84.

At school Bula is asked to draw a pig. His drawing:

The teacher comments:
—You began all right, but where's the body?
—That's set aside for export.

For another Romanian version, see Brunvand, 1973:184–85. For other versions see Durocher, 1965:23, and Meyer, 1978:66.

A VIP from India is visiting Romania. The tourist agency O.N.T. Carpati is intent on meeting any wish of the distinguished guest. The guide and interpreter asks him what his favorite dish is so that he can order it ahead at the restaurant.

—Oh, don't bother. I can just as well eat any of your national dishes. Anyway, I can't imagine how you could manage in your country to get the necessary ingredients for a specifically Indian dish.

—I assure you O.N.T. Carpati can provide anything for its distinguished guests, so please tell us what your favorite dish is.

—Well, if you insist, it's elephant ear with onion sauce. But I won't mind at all if you can't . . .

—That's all right, you'll have it for dinner.

That same afternoon, the guest catches a glimpse of an elephant in the hotel's backyard, and he is full of admiration for Romanian hospitality. However, at dinner the head waiter apologizes for not having been able to prepare the special dish for lack of ingredients.

—But I saw . . .

—Oh, there was no problem about the elephant; what we couldn't drum up was the onion.

This is no joke for people who for long periods of time had to manage cooking without either onion or garlic. At one time, when the shortage had been of particularly long duration, many individuals actually requested passports for organized one-day trips to Bulgaria just to purchase garlic. For a Czech version of the joke, see Beckmann, 1969:109. For other versions, see Winick, 1964:58, and Durocher, 1965:30–31.

There are many jokes about shortages of fundamental items. One reported in Romania in 1952 goes as follows: A Russian was recently telling a Romanian how Russia would finally deal with the United States. 'All we shall have to do,' he said, 'is pack twenty atomic bombs into twenty leather suitcases and place them strategically throughout the United States.' The Romanian shook his head dubiously. 'Don't you believe we have atomic bombs?' the Russian asked him. 'Of course,' the Romanian answered. 'The problem is, where are you going to get twenty leather suitcases?' See "A Problem of Packaging," *News from Behind the Iron Curtain*, 1, no. 12 (December, 1952): 51. For other versions of this joke, see Dor and Federmann, 1964:224; Winick, 1964:37; Kolasky, 1972:69; Benton and Loomes, 1976:101; Isnard, 1977:97–98; Paruit, 1978:108; and Kalina, 1980:250.

A young girl, on the point of drowning, cries for help. A man jumps into the water and brings her safely to shore. The girl wants to show her gratitude.

—You have saved my life. You may ask of me anything you want.

—May I ask for a night of yours?

I didn't mean it that way, but I've promised, so now I have no choice. Granted.

He takes her to a restaurant, then to a theater. They get out of the theater towards midnight. They stroll down two blocks. Then he stops near a small group of people forming a line.

—Now, since you promised, would you be so kind as to take a place in this line to get me tomorrow morning my potato ration for the coming winter.

For other versions, see Isnard, 1977:85 and Melor, 1979:30–31.

In a shoe store a customer, taking advantage of "politeness week" indulged in being choosy about the merchandise she wanted. After the vendor brought her a sample of all he had in his (poor) stock, she still wasn't satisfied.
—This shoe would be all right if you had it in brown.
—Sorry, ma'am, we only have it in black. What about this one?
—I like it, but the fit isn't perfect. Could I have it in a wider size?
—Sorry, ma'am. We only have one width.
The lady still doesn't give up and asks to try on everything available. Eventually, the vendor, unused to offering this kind of service, loses patience:
—Madam, would you please be kind enough to take my place so that I could be in your place and get myself screwed?

In order to understand this joke, one must realize that because of the permanent shortages and the lack of competition between different stores, all vendors treat customers very rudely, worse than if they were begging instead of buying. In response to numerous complaints, the government occasionally institutes a so-called week of politeness when vendors are supposedly obliged to behave in a manner which would be a minimum requirement in any civilized country but which is unusual in Communist countries. One must keep in mind that salesmen receive the same salary regardless of whether or not they sell many or few items. In short, there is little incentive for sales personnel to worry about customer relations!

—When we achieve socialism, every citizen will have his own car. When we achieve communism, every citizen will have his own helicopter.
—Why would anyone need his own helicopter?
—What a silly question! Suppose they're selling butter in Timisoara or eggs in Iasi. You'd climb in your helicopter, fly over, and buy what you need.

Timisoara and Iasi are Romanian cities a few hundred miles distant from Bucharest and from each other. One finds considerable variation in this popular joke with respect to where one flies and for what reason. For a Romanian version in which one uses one's own plane to fly to Moscow to see if one can buy some bread there, see "The Wild Blue Future," *East Europe,* 7, no. 4 (April, 1958): 30. For another Romanian text in which helicopters will be used to seek vegetables, see Meyer, 1978:78. For a Czech version in which one can fly to Prague to get a good place in the line for meat, see Beckmann, 1969:108. For a Bulgarian version in which one uses a helicopter to fly to Varna for flour or lard, see anon., 1977:940. Most versions are set in Russia. The object sought may be meat (Paruit, 1978:107); potatoes (Isnard, 1977:72; Draitser, 1978:19); sugar (Kukin, 1962:[96]; Drozdzynski, 1974:33); margarine (Brandt, 1965:74); matches (Dor and Federmann, 1964:212; Winick, 1964:60–61; Benton and Loomes, 1976:91; Kalina, 1980:173); wicks for oil lamps (Durocher, 1965:42–43); razor blades (Hirche, 1964:288); shoes (Swearingen, 1961:23); or unspecified (Kolasky, 1972:128).

At school the teacher explains the progress in the economic and social organization of the country.
—Bula, what kind of a society did we build in our country?
The multilaterally developed socialist society.
—Very well, and what did we have before that?
—Cooking oil and sugar.

"Multilaterally developed socialist society" is the term concocted by Ceausescu to mark his opposition to the Soviet-inspired COMECOM principle according to which each satellite was required to specialize in only one economic field (e.g., Romania in agriculture). The system was designed to keep all the satellites dependent upon one another and mainly upon the Soviet Union. It should also be noted that the shortage of cooking oil and sugar sometimes lasts for months at a time.

In a food store in Bucharest.
—Do you have frankfurters?
—No.
—Do you have ham?
—No.
—Do you have bologna?

—No.
—Do you have dry salami?
—No.
—Do you have . . .
—No.
After the customer leaves the store, the vendor exclaims in amazement: —What a memory!

For Czech versions, see anon., 1977:940 and Paruit, 1978:113. For Polish versions see Larsen, 1980:90, and Kalina, 1980:132.

Question for Radio Erevan.
—Why is there no flour on the market?
—Because they began adding it to bread.

For a Russian version, see Kolasky, 1972:91.

Question for Radio Erevan.
—Would it be possible to introduce socialism into the Sahara?
—In principle, yes, but after the first five-year plan, the Sahara will have to import sand.

For a Czech version, see "The Economic Drift," *East Europe,* vol. 18, no. 8–9 (August–September, 1969): 49. In a variant form, we find "When will the Cubans be certain that they have achieved socialism? When they begin importing sugar." (Kolasky, 1972:132). However, the most common version involves sand. For example, "What would happen if the Russians occupied the Sahara? For the first fifty years, nothing, but then sand would become scarce." (Hirche, 1977:143). For additional "sand" texts, see Swoboda, 1969:36; Kolasky, 1972:132; Drozdzynski, 1974:91; Isnard, 1977:16–17; Meyer, 1978:76; Paruit, 1978:197; Beckmann, 1980:96; Kalina, 1980:154; and Larsen, 1980:95.

During the first five-year plan, an American visitor was invited into the office of the director of a model factory. The American asked:
—Is productivity increasing?
—Oh, yes. During the first year we produced only five thousand, but

in the second year we produced fifty thousand, and the third year five hundred thousand. This year we'll probably make a million.
—That is impressive. May I ask what it is that you are producing?
The director reached out to the conveyor belt and pulled off a little brass tag for the visitor to inspect. It read: "The elevator isn't running."

For a Czech version, see Beckmann, 1969:118. For earlier versions, see Wolfe, 1951:13; Winick, 1964:29; and Durocher, 1965:16. For another version (in which the placard says "No meat"), see Isnard, 1977:101; for another (in which the sign says "Out of order"), see Hirche, 1964:250 and Paruit, 1978:102–3; for another (in which the enamel sign says "Watch out for falling plaster"), see Kalina, 1980:154–55.

With so many foreign tourists in the country going around shopping, vendors have been instructed to do their best to cover up shortages by offering a substitute form of merchandise in place of the item requested. A tourist enters a shop in Bucharest and asks for toilet paper.
—I'm sorry, we're out of it, but if you wish, we can offer you some excellent sandpaper.

Considering the poor quality of Romanian-made toilet paper, the suggested substitution wouldn't have made all that much difference. Anyone travelling eastward through Europe may well have noticed, from Austria on, the increasingly inferior quality of toilet paper. Admittedly there may be cultural differences in the type of paper deemed desirable. Still the existence of the joke itself is prima facie evidence of the discontent both about the shortage of such a necessity and the quality of the product when it is in stock.

In Russia, a father tells his son:
—Go to the newsstand and bring back Pravda *for me,* The Soviet Woman *for your mother,* Komsomolskaya Pravda *for you, and the* Pensioneer's Gazette *for granny.*
The kid starts to go, but on the street he runs into granny.
—Where are you going?
—To the newsstand. Dad told me to buy Pravda *for him,* The Soviet Woman *for mom,* Komsomolskaya Pravda *for me, and the* Pensioneer's Gazette *for you.*
—What's the use of buying all those papers? You read the same thing

in all of them anyway. Might as well watch TV; still the same. Forget it.
Come along with me.

Later at home, the father asks:

—Did you buy what I told you?

—No, because granny said we can get from TV all there is in the
newspapers.

—Now look here. You will do as I tell you. Get Pravda *for me,* The
Soviet Woman *for your mother,* Komsomolskaya Pravda *for you, and*
as for granny, if she prefers it, she may use the TV antenna instead of
toilet paper.

––––––––––––

—What do you think about Scanteia?

—It's an excellent newspaper.

—And Romania Libera?

—Very good, too.

—What about Lumea?

—Oh, this one isn't any good. Its paper is too thick. It clogs the
toilet.

––––––––––––

—How are things in Romania under communist rule?

—Wonderful. We live like on permanent Yom Tov.

—What do you mean?

—Well, you see, we dress like on Purim, are housed like on Sukkot,
and eat like on Yom Kippur.

Yom Tov is the Jewish word for holiday. According to tradition, there
is a carnival on Purim (when strange costumes are worn); on Sukkot
people build primitive huts out of branches; and Yom Kippur is "the
day of atonement" during which people fast.

––––––––––––

Gheorghiu-Dej, distressed by the bad shape of the Romanian econ-
omy and unable to solve the housing shortage, seeks the advice of a
rabbi.

—You know, says the rabbi, it's all only a matter of borders.

—What do you mean?

—It's simple. You can solve the housing problem by opening the
borders to the West, and the food problem by closing the border to the
East [Soviet Union].

For Hungarian versions, see "Way Out," *News from Behind the Iron Curtain,* 3, no. 3 (March, 1954): 26; Dor and Federmann, 1964:272; Drozdzynski, 1974:197; Benton and Loomes, 1976:128; Isnard, 1977:22–23; and Melor, 1979:59–60. For Czech versions, see Beckmann, 1980:102, and Kalina, 1980:25. For other versions, see Hirche, 1964:276; Durocher, 1965:30; Meyer, 1978:71; and Paruit, 1978:180–81.

The optimist:
—*If things go on like this in our socialist economy, we will all be reduced to begging.*
The pessimist:
—*Who from?*

5
It's a Wonderful Life

Under a huge slogan on a wall which reads:
"COMMUNISM SHINES LIKE THE SUN"
someone has scribbled with chalk:
"until we all get sunburnt"

For a Czech version, see Kolasky, 1972:27.

———————————

A French politician is visiting Poland. On Sunday he expresses a wish to go to church, and so, of course, an important official is assigned to accompany him.
—Are you a Catholic? asks the Frenchman.
—Believer, but not practicing.
—Of course, since you are a communist.
—Practicing, but not a believer.

For other versions, see Hirche, 1964:300; Brandt, 1965:210; Durocher, 1965:101; and Paruit, 1978:76.

———————————

What's the difference between capitalism and communism?
In capitalism, man exploits man. In communism, it's the other way round.

This has been called one of the oldest Soviet jokes. See Shenker, 1978:9. For Polish versions, see Langnas, 1963:20, and Larsen, 1980:91. For East German versions, see Dor and Federmann, 1964:155, and Brandt, 1965:150–51; for Czech versions, see Beckmann, 1969:104; Swoboda, 1969:41; and Filip and Steiger, 1977:20.

For additional versions, see Kukin, 1962:[30]; Hirche, 1964:228; Winick, 1964:24; Durocher, 1965:117; Jacobi, 1965:94; Schiff, 1969:45; Kolasky, 1972:64; Speier, 1975:72; Benton and Loomes, 1976:141; anon., 1977:67; Paruit, 1978:15; and Melor, 1979:222.

What's the difference between socialism and capitalism?
Capitalism makes social mistakes [referring to the class system and other forms of social inequality], and socialism makes capital [i.e., large] mistakes.

For other versions, see Dor and Federmann, 1964:145; Brandt, 1965:151, 246; Parth and Schiff, 1972:46; Hirche, 1977:67; and Melor, 1979:54. There are other jokes playing upon the word "capital." For example, "What did Marx bequeath to the Germans?" "To the East Germans socialism; to the West Germans [the] capital." See Jacobi, 1965:99.

—Is there anything in common between the capitalist and socialist economies?
—Yes, they both exploit capital, only in socialism man is the most important capital.

—What's the difference between capitalism and socialist economic planning?
—Under capitalism there is rigid discipline in production and chaos in consumption. Under socialist economic planning there is chaos in production and discipline in consumption.

For a Polish version, see Dor and Federmann, 1964:248. For another version set in Poland, see Benton and Loomes, 1976:98.

What's the difference between science, idealistic philosophy, and materialist (Marxist) philosophy?
—Science is like chasing a black cat in a dark room, without knowing whether it's there or not.
—Idealistic philosophy is like chasing, blindfolded, in a dark room, a black cat that isn't there.
—Materialist philosophy is like chasing, blindfolded, in a dark room,

*a black cat that isn't there, while shouting at the top of your lungs:
"I've got it!"*

For other versions, see "Problems of Philosophy," *East Europe,* 10,
no. 6 (June, 1961): 39; Dor and Federmann, 1964:265; Hirche, 1964:292;
Brandt, 1965:118; Durocher, 1965:77; Drozdzynski, 1974:160; Meyer,
1978:33; and Paruit, 1978:164.

---

*In Hungary little Moricka (Maurice) was a clever Jewish schoolboy.
In school one day the teacher gives every child a picture of Marx.
—Go home and put it somewhere and tomorrow tell the class what
you did with it.
The next day the teacher asks the children where they put their
pictures. First he asks Johnny who answers.
—I put it in the kitchen.
—Why?
—So that Marx could see how well the workers eat in a socialist
country.
Next the teacher asks Paul.
—I put the picture right over my parents' closet.
—Why?
—So that Marx could see how well the workers dress in a socialist
country.
Next the teacher asks Moricka.
—I put the picture right over my parents' bed.
—Why?
—So that Marx could see how the workers of the world unite.*

---

*A university professor of international fame has always managed to
find excuses for refusing to join the party whenever he was asked to do
so. Finally one day the party secretary followed by a group of students
and faculty members burst into his office:
—Congratulations, comrade professor. Your application to join the
party has been approved.
—But I never made any such application.
—Never mind, you make one now. Just sign this form.*

Joining the party sometimes becomes quite unavoidable when it is
deemed expedient by the party. Often the party wishes to enroll a
prestigious name perhaps to serve as a figurehead or window dressing.

Party membership may also be prescribed as a means of making emigration more difficult for an individual considered important in the economy of the country. The above story may not be very meaningful to Western readers, but it is *authentic,* and it reflects a genuine issue.

—*Hi, Ion, I've heard you got into the party.*
Ion, startled, raises his foot and looks in alarm at his heel.
—*What did you say I got into?*

In colloquial Romanian, "I was admitted to" translates very much like "I stepped into." One must know this in order to understand the above joke which is much more effective when acted out in front of an audience. In a Russian version (Kolasky, 1972:54), a note explains that the same word *Vstupat* is used in Russian to denote both "to join" and "to step into something."

—*Do you know what this is?*

—*?!?!?*
—*It's the same thing as this:*

after a trade union meeting.

In a Czech version, the droodle represents the "bottom of a listener to a speech by Novotny" before and after the speech. See Beckmann, 1969:99. A word of explanation about trade unions in communist countries is perhaps in order. Trade unions are by statute "organizations of the working people having the aim of carrying out the political line of the Communist party among and by means of non-party members." As such, in contrast to trade unions in capitalist countries, they are *not* organizations representing the interests of workers with respect to employers. For example, strikes are illegal—since supposedly the factories are "owned by the people," and who would want to strike against himself?

Since membership in the trade union of any given institution (agency, factory, research laboratory, etc.) is mandatory, the indoctrination of the entire active population is carried out in the so-called trade union meetings at which attendance is compulsory. These meetings are intended to achieve other ends as well. They are designed to browbeat people into obedience—everyone has to approve items on the agenda by applauding and cheering on command. They tend to create the false impression of popular participation in political life inasmuch as suggestions are apparently coming from the masses. (In practice, individuals are instructed carefully as to when to suggest what, according to party directives.) At these meetings, many people make long speeches even if they have essentially nothing to say. The idea is simply to put on a show of popular enthusiasm for a proposed party-inspired decision or for a nominated candidate in one of the "free elections." Trade union speeches provide a good platform for promotion—both political and professional.

A well-known Romanian mathematician, a member of the Romanian Academy of Sciences, once surprised his friends by saying:

—You know, I'm becoming superstitious. I'm beginning to believe in dream omens.

—You, professor! Impossible!

—Oh yes, I've noticed that dreams come true. I once had a dream that I was at a meeting of the Academy. Then I woke up. And I really was at a meeting at the Academy.

For versions told about a party meeting, see Paruit, 1978:71–72, and Kalina, 1980:87.

There is a trade union meeting. At the end of a long speech about the steady increase in the general standard of living, the group is invited to participate in a question and answer period. Popescu asks:

—Before the war meat was easily available, but now we can get it only after hours of queuing. Where is all our meat?

—I'm sorry, comrade, but I cannot answer your question right away since I do not have the meat statistics with me. I'll look them up, and I will answer you next week.

Next week there is another meeting. Popescu raises his hand again.

—Why can't we find for weeks at a time any vegetable oil? Where is all our oil?

Same kind of answer. Two weeks later there is another meeting. This time, Ionescu raises his hand.

—I have one question. Where is my friend Popescu?

For Hungarian versions, see Sanders, 1962:25; Kukin, 1962:[130]; Jacobi, 1965:13; and Lo Bello, 1966:24. For Czech versions, see Beckmann, 1969:21, and Filip and Steiger, 1977:25; for Polish versions, see Drozdzynski, 1974:114; and Melor, 1979:134–35. For an East German version, see Brandt, 1965:95–96; for Russian versions, see Winick, 1964:27, and Dolgopolova, 1982:31. For a version set in Yugoslavia, see Meyer, 1978:82–83. For a Modern Greek version, see Orso, 1979:10. For additional versions, see Hirche, 1964:295; Durocher, 1965:138–39; anon., 1977:850; Paruit, 1978:79; and Kalina, 1980:136.

It is 1948. A man is being indoctrinated by his friend.

—Do you know who Vasile Luca is?

—No, I don't.

—And do you know who Chivu Soica is?

—No, I don't.

—And do you know who Patrascanu is?

—No, I don't.

—You see, if instead of spending all of your time at home, you'd come to party meetings, you'd be better informed about what's happening in our country.

—But do you know who Simionescu is?

—No, this time you got me.

—You see, if instead of spending all your time at party meetings, you'd stay more at home, you'd know that Simionescu is the man your wife is having an affair with.

For a version from Yugoslavia, see Jacobi, 1965:141. For a Czech version, see Filip and Steiger, 1977:34. For Polish versions, see Drozdzynski, 1974:130–31; Levy, 1976:22; Hirche 1977:154–55; and Melor, 1979:158.

At a factory trade union meeting, the lecture is again on the improved living conditions of the workers in Romania under communist rule. At the end the lecturer says:

—We shall now take a few examples from your own lives, comrades.

Let's see, comrade Popescu, come over here. Are you satisfied with your living conditions as compared with those in the past?

—Oh, sure I am.

—Be more specific. Please answer all my questions by comparing what you have now and what you had before. What about your housing space?

—I now have a four-room apartment with kitchen and bathroom. Before we used to live, the whole family, in just one room, without kitchen and with only a toilet.

—Excellent. You see, comrades, what our government and our party are doing for the people? And how are you eating now?

—We eat meat daily, and also fresh fruit and vegetables, and cookies. Before we ate only dried brown bread, cabbage and beans, and only on holidays could we afford meat.

—Excellent. You see, comrades, what our government and our party are doing for the people. And under the present conditions, are you able to save?

—Sure. My savings account is increasing slowly but steadily. By contrast, in the past I was up to my neck in debts.

—Now I want you to tell so that everyone can hear when this wonderful change in your life occurred.

—Right after my daughter started her love affair with the town's party secretary.

For other versions, see Kukin, 1962:[29]; Dor and Federmann, 1964:223–25; Durocher, 1965:24–25; Jacobi, 1965:40; Benton and Loomes, 1976:81–82; and Melor, 1979:153–54.

A raven stands on a branch of a tree holding a piece of bread in its beak. A fox comes by and tries to get the bread by means of the old trick.

—How beautiful you are! I suppose your voice is equally pleasant. Will you sing something for me?

The raven is educated by now and has read the old fable. He puts the bread under his wing, crows, and then retrieves the bread.

The fox tries something else.

—I'm sorry, but as a friend I feel it's my duty to let you know that your wife is fooling around with the party secretary of the forest.

The raven opens its beak in surprise and drops the bread. The fox picks it up greedily and goes away.

Moral: When your wife is fooling around with the party secretary, keep your mouth shut or you'll lose your bread.

This is a modern version of an Aesopic fable. Specifically, it is Aarne-Thompson tale type 57, Raven with Cheese in his Mouth. For a Polish version of this contemporary form of the story, see "The Crow and the Fox," *East Europe,* 6, no. 6 (June, 1957): 62. For a Czech version, see Beckmann, 1969:26. For another version, see Melor, 1979:156–57.

A man enters a pet shop to buy a parrot.
—How much is this parrot?
—Five hundred lei.
—What can it do?
—It can speak 5 words.
—And the one over there?
—It costs 700 lei. It can speak whole phrases.
—And this one?
—This is 1500. It can speak French too.
—And how much is this one?
—5,000 lei.
—Heavens! What can it speak to cost so much?
—Oh, it does not speak at all, but it's the party secretary.

For other versions, see Drozdzynski, 1974:154, and Kalina, 1980:156. Party secretaries need no qualifications, do not work very hard, but receive the highest pay.

There's an opening for a high office at the Ministry of Foreign Affairs. Three candidates have applied. One has a Ph.D. in political science from the University of Moscow, another is a specialist in international law, and the third one is an old diplomat with many years of service and who can speak four foreign languages. Who got the job?
—Ceausescu's cousin.

For other Romanian versions see Drozdzynski, 1974:208, and Kalina, 1980:136–37.

The Romanian minister of transportation visits his Soviet counterpart. He is surprised to see the luxurious house and his rich lifestyle, much more than one would expect for a party member of his rank.
—How do you manage? he asks.
The Soviet minister takes him to the window.

—*Do you see that bridge over there?*
—*Yes.*
—*Well, that bridge cost one hundred million rubles. And from such a large sum a little bit comes my way.*
A few years later, the Soviet minister of transportation returns the visit. The lifestyle of the Romanian minister is even more lavish.
—*How do you manage?*
—*You see that bridge over there?*
—*What bridge?*
—*Well, that bridge too cost one hundred million lei.*

For a version set in Hungary, see Paruit, 1978:120. For another version, see Kalina, 1980:255–56.

At a political meeting, a speaker has given a long lecture full of propaganda praising the permanent improvement in living standards, followed by a comparison between the miserable salaries of workers in the capitalist world and the good salaries of working people in socialist countries. At the end of the presentation, he asks:
—*Are there any questions or comments?*
—*I I I have s s s something to to to s s say.*
—*Go ahead!*
—*L l long l l live c c comrade Gheorghiu-D D Dej*
—*Bravo, bravo. . . . (ten minutes of cheers and applause).*
—*Anybody else want to speak?*
—*I I I haven't f f f finished, c c comrade.*
—*All right, go ahead!*
—*L l long l l live c c comrade Gheorghiu-D D Dej on my s s salary!*

For a Polish version, see "Political Laughter in Poland," *East Europe,* 18, no. 1 (January, 1969):25. For a Russian version, see Winick, 1964:43.

An American worker falls in love with a Romanian girl, and he takes a job in a factory in Bucharest. He comes each morning exactly when he is supposed to, he works very hard until ten, he eats his sandwich in fifteen minutes, and continues his work. Around him, the other workers work as they always do. When payday comes, the American receives the normal amount, that is, the same as that given to all the workers. He says:
—*I didn't participate in the strike so why am I given strike pay?*

This joke includes the stereotype of the American eating quickly and working hard, but the real commentary is on the pay scale. One revealing folk slogan in Romania makes much the same point: "Our country pretends to pay us and we pretend to work." For another version of this joke, also set in Romania, see Meyer, 1978:64. For a Czech version of the slogan, see Beckmann, 1980:98.

At a factory, a special party meeting is called.
—Comrades, a class enemy is in our midst. We must increase our vigilance in order to unmask him.
Ionescu raises his hand.
—Trust me, comrades. I'm sure I can unmask him at our next trade union meeting.
At the next trade union meeting, long and tedious speeches are delivered as usual. When the meeting is over, Ionescu says to the secretary of the party organization:
—I know who the class enemy is. It's X. . .
—How did you find out?
—By simply applying the teachings of Marxism-Leninism which show us that the class enemy never sleeps. Well, X. . . was the only one who didn't sleep at the meeting.

For East German versions, see Hirche, 1964:242–43, and Abrahams and Wukasch, 1967:9; for Czech versions, see Filip and Steiger, 1977:49, and Kalina, 1980:87; for a Hungarian version, see Aranyossy, 1971:101. For additional versions, see Durocher, 1965:83; Kolasky, 1972:71; Paruit, 1978:77–78; and Melor, 1979:161. In a variant, the Poles are said to have stopped producing beds because they were not needed: the dead sleep in cemeteries, the peasants sleep on straw, workers sleep at meetings, students sleep at lectures, soldiers rest on their laurels, the party is on constant guard, and the enemy never sleeps. See Kolasky, 1972:40. In an East German text: Why don't they make beds any more in the German Democratic Republic? The intellectuals are lying in a bed of roses; the activists are resting on their laurels; the workers and peasants are on permanent alert; the class enemy never sleeps. All the others are either standing trial or sitting out their sentences. See Benton and Loomes, 1976:104, and Brandt, 1965:41, 98–99.

A Romanian trade union leader is visiting Great Britain. After he has toured several industrial towns, an English trade unionist asks him:

—What are your impressions of British industry?

—I'm quite amazed at the way you trade unionists behave in this country. In Romania strikes or work disputes are unheard of. Workers give their best; they even put in extra hours without asking for extra pay. No worker would ever think of pursuing his own petty interests at the expense of the state's goals.

—Well, if you can afford to do that, it is clear that you don't have any communists in your trade unions to cause trouble.

For other versions, see Benton and Loomes, 1976:19–20; Paruit, 1978:77; and Larsen, 1980:88. The paradox in this joke is only apparent. In Romania, there are no Communists, only party members. The old Communists have either been exterminated by Stalinist purges or have long since become disillusioned. As to trade unions, the term carries quite a different meaning in Communist countries than in capitalist ones.

About one month after a miners' strike, a news item appeared in the Romanian daily Scanteia:

Comrade Ceausescu has visited the coal mines in the Jiu Valley where he gave a talk on domestic freedoms in front of an enthusiastic audience. The miners acclaimed him by shaking their chains.

For another version, see Paruit, 1978:187. The joke, of course, is commenting on the fact that strikes are forbidden. The leaders of the miners' strike were not put in chains but were jailed. The unprecedented strike in Poland in August 1980 underscores the irony that free trade unions with the right to strike are not permitted in supposedly workers' states.

—When did the first free elections take place?

—When God made Eve out of one of Adam's ribs and then told him: Choose a wife.

In Romania, as in the Soviet Union, elections consist of folding the single list of candidates and placing it in the ballot box. This is what communist propaganda calls "free elections." For other versions of the joke, see Kukin, 1962:[132]; Schiff, 1969:60; Swoboda, 1969:12; Kolasky, 1972:124; Drozdzynski, 1974:207; Benton and Loomes, 1976:141; Paruit, 1978:78–79; Melor, 1979:138; Kalina, 1980:178; and Larsen, 1980:94.

After the first "free elections," two Romanians are discussing the outcome.

—*Isn't it extraordinary, 99.5 percent of the population has voted for our communist leaders.*

—*Yes, but what's even more extraordinary is that I keep meeting only the 0.5 percent.*

For a version set in Nazi Germany (1938), see Benton and Loomes, 1976:65. For other versions, see Kukin, 1962:[88]; Brandt, 1965:178; Durocher, 1965:54; and Kalina, 1980:178.

Two friends meet in the street.

—*What's the matter with you, Petre? Why are you so dejected?*

—*I t t tried to g g get a a a new j j job and I w w was t t turned d d down.*

—*Why? What kind of a job was it?*

—*It w w was as an an n n ouncer at the rad d dio st st station, and they s s said I c c couldn't g g get the j j job b b because I'm n n not a p p party m m member.*

For another Romanian version, see Drozdzynski, 1974:204. For a version from Yugoslavia, see Dor and Federmann, 1964:287. For another version, see Paruit, 1978:164. This joke is reported in the West. In a Jewish text, a stuttering complainant claims he didn't get a radio sportscaster job because of anti-Semitism. See Richard M. Dorson, "Jewish-American Dialect Stories on Tape," in Raphael Patai, Francis Lee Utley, and Dov Noy, eds., *Studies in Biblical and Jewish Folklore* (Bloomington: Indiana University Press, 1960), 144–45.

Ionescu runs into his friend Popescu soon after the latter had joined the Communist party.

—*Hi, so nice to see you. Let's go somewhere for a drink.*

—*Sorry, I can't. I'm off to a party meeting.*

—*When then can we meet for a drink?*

—*I don't know. Tomorrow I have another party meeting and another the day after tomorrow.*

—*Couldn't we perhaps meet after the meeting?*

—*Impossible. These meetings last until late into the night.*

—*But when do you manage to sleep, then?*

—*At the party meetings.*

Question for Radio Erevan.
—Can one sit down on a hedgehog?
—In principle yes, if the party asks you to.

In an earlier version, Radio Erevan informs its listeners that there are only two occasions when it is comfortable to sit on a hedgehog. "The first is when the animal has been shaved. The second is when the party orders you to do it." See Sulzberger, 1962:32. In another version, Ho Chi Minh is asked in 1951 at the time of one of his trips to Moscow if it were possible to sit on a hedgehog. He answers in principle, no, but there are three exceptions: if one shaves the hedgehog, if one asks someone else to sit in his place, and if the party orders it. See Meyer, 1978:83. For other versions, see Winick, 1964:49; Jacobi, 1965:95; Schiff, 1969:74; Kalina, 1980:88; and Dolgopolova, 1982:122.

—Can one define what a communist is?
—In principle, yes, It is a man who has given up any hope of ever becoming a capitalist.

For other versions, see Hirche, 1964:294; Brandt, 1965:151; Jacobi, 1965:63; and Schiff, 1969:59.

—What is the difference between a fairy tale in the West and a fairy tale in the East?
—A fairy tale in the West starts with the words "Once upon a time there was . . ." A fairy tale in the East starts with the words "Once upon a time there will be . . ."

For other versions, see Hirche, 1964:289; Brandt, 1965:246; Schiff, 1969:60; Swoboda, 1969:58; Benton and Loomes, 1976:144; Melor, 1979:40; and Kalina, 1980:178. In one version, the initial question is: "what is the difference between a fairy tale and a Soviet economic plan?" A tale begins with "one day there was," and the Soviet plan begins with "one day there will be." See Drozdzynski, 1974:41.

Ivan dies and his soul is directed to hell. In front of the gate a devil asks him:
—Do you want to go to the capitalist hell or to the communist hell?
Ivan hesitates, puzzled, when he hears his friend Vasili hailing him from behind the gate.

—Hi, Ivan, come on in to our hell; in the capitalist hell they'll throw you into a huge cauldron full of boiling tar where you will burn eternally.

—And in the socialist hell?

—The arrangement is the same, only here they either run short of tar, or they run short of fuel, and when both fuel and tar are available, the devils have a trade union meeting.

For earlier Romanian versions of this popular joke, see "Burning Choice," *East Europe,* vol. 6, no. 4 (April, 1957): 10; Julian Hale, *Ceausescu's Romania: A Political Documentary* (London: George G. Harrap, 1971), 69; and Brunvand, 1973:186. For Czech versions, see Beckmann, 1969:105; Swoboda, 1969:37–38; Filip and Steiger, 1977:30; Kalina, 1980:188. For a Hungarian version, see Drozdzynski, 1974:194. For Polish versions, see Hirche, 1977:155–56; Isnard, 1977:26. For an East German version, see Larsen, 1980:94–95. For additional versions, see Sulzberger, 1962:32; Winick, 1964:10–11; Kolasky, 1972:128–29; Parth and Schiff, 1972:77; Benton and Loomes, 1976:154; Meyer, 1978:68; Paruit, 1978:16; and Dolgopolova, 1982:23.

Two men meet on the street.

—How are you doing?

—Could be worse. Both me and my wife have good jobs. My mother-in-law lives with us and takes care of the children when they come home from school. All in all, we lead a good enough life.

—How do you manage? I have a family of four, and although both me and my wife have very well-paid jobs and I also work extra hours, we can hardly make ends meet.

—You see, I have an uncle in America, and he sends us from time to time a gift package. By selling its contents, we add a substantial amount to our income.

—That's great. But then your uncle must be a rich man, a dirty capitalist.

—Oh no, he lives on unemployment.

For an early version of this joke, see Dallin, 1949:15; For other Romanian versions, see Kukin, 1962:[143]; Benton and Loomes, 1976:116; and Melor, 1979:52–53. For other versions, see Hirche, 1964:264; Isnard, 1977:55–56; and Meyer, 1978:74–75.

A peasant was called upon to contribute ten thousand lei to the latest state loan. The peasant was concerned about what might happen to his money. He asked an official:
—*Who guarantees that I shall ever get it back?*
—*Our beloved comrade, Ana Pauker, answered the official.*
—*Yes, but what if she dies?*
—*Then the party will guarantee your money.*
The peasant remained sceptical.
—*Yes, but what if the party is dissolved?*
The official, annoyed, threw down his pen.
—*You lout, wouldn't it be worth losing ten thousand lei for that?*

For another version from Romania, see "No Guarantee," *News from Behind the Iron Curtain*, 1, no. 3 (March, 1952): 43. For a version about Khrushchev and a price of five hundred rubles, see Kukin, 1962:[56]. For a version with one thousand rubles, see Parth and Schiff, 1972:66. For a version set in Poland, see Dolgopolova, 1982:37. For a summary account of the details of the career of Ana Pauker, see "The Rise and Fall of Ana Pauker," *News from Behind the Iron Curtain*, 1, no. 7 (July, 1952): 16–21.

Two friends meet.
—*Since you are working at S.P.C. [State Planning Committee], maybe you could explain to me what's the meaning of mandatory profits in the dealings between the two government agencies.*
—*It's hard to define, but let me tell you a story. A man is walking a dog on a leash when he meets a friend.*
—*Where are you going with that dog?*
—*I'm trying to sell it.*
—*For how much?*
—*Twenty thousand dollars.*
—*Are you crazy? Who do you think will give you twenty thousand dollars for a dog?*
—*Well, I'm going to try anyway.*
After a while, the two friends meet again.
—*Did you sell your dog?*
—*Sure I did.*
—*For how much?*
—*As I told you, twenty thousand dollars.*
—*Oh, come on, did you really get all that money for a dog?*

—Well, not exactly, but I got in exchange two cats worth ten thousand dollars each.

For other versions, see Durocher, 1965:44, 46; Drozdzynski, 1974:138; and Melor, 1979:62.

A kid trying to sell his sunflower seeds shouts:
—Nylon seeds, nylon seeds.
—Stop this nonsense, says a passerby. You know there's no such thing as nylon seeds.
—But doesn't the newspaper boy in the next block shout: Free Romania?

Before Romania started to produce its own supply of synthetic materials, nylon was a very rare and highly appreciated commodity, available only through import. *Free Romania* is a Romanian newspaper. There are other jokes which play on the names of newspapers. For example, in an East German text, a West German overhears the following exchange at a Leipzig newsstand. "A *Neues Deutschland [New(s) Germany].*" "It's not yet here." "Then please *Die Freiheit [Freedom]*!" "That will only come together with the *Neuen Deutschland.*" Hirche, 1964:260.

—What's the difference between a tomato and a member of the Communist party?
—There's isn't any. They both turn red after having been green first.

In order to understand this joke, one needs to know that many of Romania's young fascists, also known as the "green shirts," sheltered themselves from prosecution at the end of World War II by joining the Communist party. This explains how the color change from green to red serves as a metaphor for the political shift from fascism to communism. In a related variant text the question is: what's the difference between a watermelon and a Romanian communist? A watermelon is green on the outside and red on the inside; a Romanian communist is red on the outside and green inside. This latter text may well be related to traditional riddles for watermelon dependent upon the same color contrast. See, for example, Archer Taylor, *English Riddles from Oral Tradition* (Berkeley and Los Angeles: University of California Press, 1951), 558–59, 625, 632 (riddles 1376, 1508, and 1547 in particular).

Larsen (1980:44) reports a text which dates from the early days of the Nazi regime in Germany. In this text the color shift reflects a change from communism to fascism: what have a storm trooper and an English beefsteak in common? Both are brown outside and red inside.

—What is the definition of "exchange of opinion"?
—It's going to your boss with your own opinion and leaving with his.

For a Russian version, see Draitser, 1978:65. For another version, see Melor, 1979:218.

A delegation of party officials is visiting an asylum. As they pass by, the inmates begin to sing in their honor the popular song "It's Great to Live in Our Socialist Republic." A member of the delegation notices a man staying apart from the others and not participating in the chorus.
—Why aren't you singing with the others? he asks.
—Oh, I'm not crazy, I'm the doctor, came the answer.

For Russian versions, see Winick, 1964:15; Draitser, 1978:46. For an earlier version told about Mussolini, see Larsen, 1980:54–55. In a version from Nazi Germany, Hitler visits an insane asylum where a mass of patients renders a smart "Deutschen Gruss" (the Heil Hitler gesture). Hitler notices a few arms not raised in the salute. He asks the individuals, "Why didn't you salute me?" "My Führer, we are not lunatics; we are the attendants." See Gamm, 1979[1963]:86–87.

—Doctor, I don't feel well.
—Who does?

For other versions, see Paruit, 1978:182, and Kalina, 1980:41.

A man goes to a psychiatrist.
—Doctor, something is very wrong with me.
—What's the matter?
—Every night I dream I'm crossing the frontier illegally.
—Don't you worry, a lot of people dream that.
—Yeah, only I dream that I cross it to the east [to the Soviet Union].

For other versions, see Paruit, 1978:191–92, and Kalina, 1980:210. There are a number of jokes which employ mental illness as a convenient metaphor for a political plight. For example, "What should I do, doctor? I suffer from a split personality. I think of one thing; I say another, and I do a third." "Go to the government clinic; I don't treat members of the party." See Durocher, 1965:84–85, and Kolasky, 1972:56.

An American of Romanian origin is visiting his native country. He asks a friend:
—How is it to live in a socialist country?
—Fine. We all live like on a ship.
—What do you mean?
—Well, long-range perspectives and distant horizons are visible, and no one can get off although everyone is getting sick.

For other versions, see Winick, 1964:27; Swoboda, 1969:24; Drozdzynski, 1974:36; Filip and Steiger, 1977:33; Draitser, 1978:49; Melor, 1979:217; and Dolgopolova, 1982:42.

—Did you hear that in New York City they put up a huge poster showing in succession Marx, Engels, Lenin, and Stalin?
—How come?
—It had the caption: "From barbarism to civilization, the progress due to the Gillette blade."

A Jew is trying to escape across the border of an east European country. Unfortunately, he is caught by some frontier guards. One of them asks:
—What are you doing?
—Nothing.
—What do you mean "nothing"? You nearly crossed the frontier.
—Well, I had terrible stomach cramps, and I just had to go.
—Show me.
The poor Jew scratches around in the underbrush and finds a dog feces.
—Voilà! he says.
—But that's a dog's.
The Jew shrugs and says:
—With such a life, such a pile!

For a version in which a Czech attempts to cross over into Austria, see Paruit, 1978:116.

At a party meeting of the religious workers' organization the following interrogation takes place.

—Comrade rabbi, we've heard that you are straying from the right path. The party is worried about your deviations. Why do you eat pork?

—I was wrong, comrades, I'm exercising self-criticism.

—We also heard that you were riding on the Sabbath.

—Yes, I did once and I regret it. I'm exercising self-criticism.

—We also found out that you are frequenting, well, . . . houses . . .

—Oh!

—What do you mean, oh? We know it for a fact. Useless to deny it. You better exercise self-criticism.

—No, I meant: oh, now I know where I left my umbrella.

Of course, there is obviously no such thing as an official religious worker's organization. This joke is common enough in the West. For a representative version, see *Over Sexteen* (New York: J. M. Elgart, 1951), 14. What is interesting is the way the joke has been localized in Romania to parody self-criticism.

Ceausescu wants to know why the Romanian economy is in such bad shape. After a few unproductive discussions with his advisors, he decides to seek the counsel of a rabbi.

—Well, there are three reasons why things don't work, says the rabbi. It will be easier to explain if you come shopping with me.

They enter a department store.

—Do you have any left-handed cups? asks the rabbi.

—Sorry, we don't carry any, says the vendor, who doesn't want to be bothered.

—You see, that's the first reason, says the rabbi.

They enter another store.

—Do you have any left-handed cups?

—Well, we have a few, but of course it's going to cost you more, says the vendor, who happens to be Jewish.

He disappears for a minute and after having turned a cup around, he hands it to his customers.

—That's the second reason, says the rabbi as they leave the shop.

Ceausescu ponders a moment and then says:

—I can't make any sense of all this complication with a first and a second reason.
—That's the third reason, says the rabbi.

In a version of this joke set in Nazi times, Himmler wanted to demonstrate to Goebbels the superior commercial skills of Jews. Entering an "Aryan" shop, Himmler asks for a left-handed beer mug. The assistant apologizes, explaining there are none in stock. Later in a Jewish shop, the request is repeated. The old shopkeeper rummages about and emerges holding up a beer mug in his left hand, saying that left-handed beer mugs are quite rare and that is why they cost fifty pfennigs extra. Himmler pays and upon leaving the shop turns to Goebbels exclaiming "What did I tell you?" "What does that prove," Goebbels grumbles, "except that these damn Jews can afford to carry more stock." See Benton and Loomes, 1976:59–60.

A new airplane type has crashed several times on its test flight, each time because of a broken wing. After running out of solutions, the designer decided to consult a rabbi.
—My advice, says the rabbi, is to perforate the wing at its joint with the body of the airplane.
The designer is doubtful, but since everything else has failed, he tries it anyway. The plane flies perfectly. The designer returns to the rabbi.
—Rabbi, how did you come upon this brilliant idea?
—Oh, it was just my experience with toilet paper which never tears where it is perforated.

For another version, see Schiff, 1969:115. For an American version, see Ray Ginger, *Ray Ginger's Jokebook about American History* (New York: New Viewpoints, 1974), 86.

There is a meeting at school of parents and teachers. A teacher says:
—We must take good care of our children's education, because, you see, our generation may not live long enough to see the bright reign of communism, but our children surely will.
Somebody interrupts:
—That will serve those rascals right.

For other versions, see Jacobi, 1965:121, and Drozdzynski, 1974:164.

Three boys are reprimanded for coming to school late.
—Vasile, why are you late?
—Comrade teacher, I helped an old woman to cross the street.
—All right, you're excused. This is a good pioneer action. What
about you, Ilie?
—I also helped the old woman to cross the street.
—And you, Ionel?
—I also helped the old woman to cross the street.
—But why did it take so many of you for this good deed?
—Well, you see, comrade teacher, she *didn't* want *to cross the street.*

For an American version, see Larry Wilde, *The Official Smart Kids Joke Book* (Los Angeles: Pinnacle Books, 1977), 67. The theme of this joke is reminiscent of a communist slogan taught at indoctrination classes from grammar school on:

> If you don't know, we will teach you
> If you can't, we will help you
> If you don't want to, we will force you

Popescu, having proved both his loyalty to the party and his ability, is sent on a very important mission to Budapest. A few days after his departure, he sends the following telegram to his boss:
"Mission accomplished. Long live free and independent Hungarian Socialist Republic. Popescu."
The following week, he is sent to Czechoslovakia on a similar mission. Again he sends a telegram:
"Mission accomplished. Long live free and independent Czechoslovak Socialist Republic. Popescu."
This time he is decorated and receives the title of "hero of socialist labor." Being fully trusted after so many proofs of loyalty, he is sent to Paris. He again sends a telegram:
"Mission accomplished. Long live free and independent Popescu in Paris."

For other versions of this popular joke, see Kukin, 1962:[115]; Sulzberger, 1962:32; Dor and Federmann, 1964:214; Hirche, 1964:291; Winick, 1964:62; Durocher, 1965:65; Swoboda, 1969:35; Drozdzynski, 1974:106–7; Benton and Loomes, 1976:140; Isnard, 1977:23–24; Meyer, 1978:62; Melor, 1979:211; Kalina, 1980:125; and Dolgopolova, 1982:33.

Ceausescu visits China and is received by Mao Tse-tung who shows him all the new achievements of his country. They are all due, says Mao, to the enthusiasm of the eight hundred million Chinese for their political system.
—But aren't there also some people opposed to your regime?
—Oh, there certainly are a few. Maybe some twenty million.
—Yah, that's about the same as in Romania.

The population of Romania was at that time slightly over twenty million. For other Romanian versions of the joke, see Brunvand, 1973: 186, and Paruit, 1978: 182–83; for East German versions, see Dor and Federmann, 1964: 150; Hirche, 1964: 218–19; Abrahams and Wukasch, 1967: 8; Drozdzynski, 1974: 178–79; and Hirche, 1977: 146; for Hungarian versions, see "No Cause for Alarm," *News from Behind the Iron Curtain,* 3, no. 6 (June, 1954): 19; Jacobi, 1965: 17; and "Jokes Current in East Europe," *East Europe,* vol. 17, no. 3 (March, 1968): 49; for Czech versions, see Beckmann, 1969: 24, and Kalina, 1980: 202; for Polish versions, see Durocher, 1965: 161–62; and Kolasky, 1972: 39; for a Modern Greek version, see Larsen, 1980: 103–4.

On one of his trips to the West, Ceausescu is questioned by a reporter:
—How many Jews are there now in Romania?
—Between fifty and one hundred thousand.
—And how many wish to leave?
—Twenty million.

At school a teacher questions Bula, a student.
—Which road to socialism is the best?
—The one which takes longest, comrade teacher.

In order to assert Romania's independence from the Soviet Union, Ceausescu has defended at various international conferences the right of each nation to find its own road to socialism. The above joke plays on the choice of roads or paths. For other versions of the joke, see Durocher, 1965: 179; Benton and Loomes, 1976: 117; and Meyer, 1978: 60. Bula is not a name common in Romania, but it is often used in jokes about schoolboys.

After Romania changed its name from the Romanian Popular Republic to the Socialist Republic of Romania, two friends comment on the event:
—What do you think, Moritz, have we at this point reached 100 percent socialism, or could it get worse?

For other versions, see Kukin, 1962:[55]; Dor and Federmann, 1964:210; Winick, 1964:56; Brandt, 1965:178; Durocher, 1965:169, Benton and Loomes, 1976:90; Meyer, 1978:55; and Melor, 1979:222. In a joke on a related theme, the question is: what is the difference between an optimist and a pessimist? The pessimist says, "It is so bad that it cannot possibly get worse." The optimist says, "It can, it can." See Kolasky, 1972:113; Drozdzynski, 1974:97; and Melor, 1979:214.

Question:
—According to what we learn at the ideology courses, in a classless society money is no longer needed for the circulation of goods. Am I to understand that under communism there won't be any money?
Answer:
—Under communism too?

The joke is referring to the two separate stages of socialism and communism, the point being that there is already no money under socialism. Thus, the lack of money in the next progressive stage of communism would be nothing new. A popular variant of this joke goes as follows: Will there be any money when socialism has reached its highest level of development? In principle yes and no. There are two theories on the matter. According to one, there will be money; according to the other, there will be no money. It's also possible that a compromise solution will result: some people will have money and some people won't. In an East German text, the question "Will there be money under communism?" is answered by "No, everything has already been stolen under socialism." See Hirche, 1964:294; and Brandt, 1965:151. For other versions, see Streit, 1964:28; Schiff, 1969:55; Drozdzynski, 1974:67; Meyer, 1978:66–67; Paruit, 1978:64; and Kalina, 1980:227.

A teacher questions Bula in school:
—How far have we got with the republic?
—Five feet, eleven inches, comrade professor.

—What do you mean?
—You see, my father is five feet, ten inches, and he says he's had it up to here.

Normally, the telling of this joke is accompanied by a hand gesture in which the raconteur's hand is raised slightly above his head. In a Polish version of the joke, a schoolboy explains that Lenin was five feet tall. The teacher asks how he knows that. "Because," says the student, placing his hand on his Adam's apple, "My father is six feet tall and he says he's had it up to here with Lenin!" See Levy, 1976:25. For a Russian version in which socialism is 155 centimeters tall in comparison to a little boy's father who is 175 centimeters tall, see Drozdzynski, 1974:30. For other versions, see Jacobi, 1965:103; Swoboda, 1969:48, Isnard, 1977:12; and Melor, 1979:221.

Bula has graduated from the University of Bucharest. The job assignments are announced:
Those who have an average grade between 9.60 and ten will get jobs in Bucharest. Those between nine and 9.60 will get jobs on a radius of twenty-five miles from Bucharest . . . Those between six and 6.5 will get jobs in the Oradea area [almost four hundred miles from Bucharest, near the border].
Bula, to his crony:
—Under these conditions, I'm best off.
—How do you mean?
—With my grades between four and five, I'm sure to land a job in Frankfort [Germany].

Upon graduation from college, young people are compelled to accept the jobs that are offered them. All students prefer jobs in the big cities where living conditions are much better, but such jobs are in short supply. The principal official criteria for getting good jobs are grades, with passing grades between six and ten, and political reliability. The unofficial criteria, often more effective, are influence and bribery. The joke affirms that people try to stay as close to Bucharest as possible but that low examination scores typically lead to assignment in the provinces. In this case, Bula, with his less than satisfactory grades, is presumably hoping to be sent to Frankfort which would be freedom.

In Bucharest in April 1954 two workers have just received a layoff notice. They leave the plant, and walking outside its walls, they see, in

huge red letters, the slogan "THIS FACTORY BELONGS TO ITS
WORKERS." One of them says to the other:
—*Say, Mitica, why did we fire ourselves?*

Although communist governments boast about not having unemployment in their countries, in the early years of communism in Romania, there were occasional country-wide lay-offs, both for economic and political reasons. In the language of Newspeak, the layoffs were given the name of "compression" or "restructuration." They served as a good method of keeping people in line. In more recent times unemployment is reserved for dissidents or for individuals who have applied for emigration. It is worth remarking that since officially there is no unemployment, the notion of unemployment insurance does not exist in these countries.

A Western trade union delegation is visiting the Soviet Union. At a
factory the chief of the delegation asks the manager:
—*How many people work in this factory?*
—*Half, at most, came the answer.*

For other versions, see anon. 1977:714; Filip and Steiger, 1977:28; Paruit, 1978:98, Shenker, 1978:9; Kalina, 1980:186.

Question:
—*A comrade has surprised his wife in bed with another man. At the*
divorce hearings, he *was considered guilty. Is this fair?*
Answer:
—*In principle, yes, for the comrade had left work too early.*

For another version, see Schiff, 1969:82.

With so many Western tourists visiting the country, the Ministry of
Foreign Trade has decided to open a special massage parlor for customers paying in hard currency. Every effort is made to set it up in a
lavish way. On the day of the official opening, the minister comes to
inspect the hostesses. He is impressed by one of them, by her educated
speech and her perfect mastery of three foreign languages. Intrigued,
he asks her:
—*Say, comrade, did you have any higher education?*
—*Sure, I hold a Ph.D. in political science.*

—Then how come you don't work in an institute of political and economic studies?

—Oh no, my mother would never allow me to go to a place like that!

The more usual version of this joke concerns joining the Communist party. For a discussion of Polish and Hungarian versions, see Sanders, 1962:22. For a Russian version in which a whore is asked why she hasn't joined the Communist party, see Draitser, 1978:13. For a Czech version, see Kalina, 1980:47.

A spaceship jointly staffed by an American, a Russian, and a Romanian is in orbit for three days. Upon its return, each of the astronauts is congratulated by the president of his country and offered a reward.

The American president:

—Would you prefer a second house or a yacht?

—Thank you, Mr. President, I already have a yacht, but I'd love a country home in which to spend my holidays with my family.

The Russian president:

—Would you prefer a car or to have a two-room apartment assigned to you?

—Thank you, Mr. President. I already have a car, but I'd be happy to move with my family into a two-room apartment.

The Romanian president:

—The party, the government, and the country are proud of you. But . . . what about those three days? Do you prefer to take them for your regular vacation or to consider them unpaid leave?

For a Polish version, see "Jokes Current in Eastern Europe," *East Europe,* 17, no. 3 (March, 1968): 48. For a Czech version, see Kalina, 1980:24.

A party official needs a secretary. After the political screening several young girls are tested professionally and by a psychologist who asks the following question:

—How much is two and two?

The first candidate answers:

—It may be four, it may be five, depends on the circumstances.

The second answers four and sticks to her answer each time the question is repeated to her. The third one falters, says four, then five, then six. The psychologist gives his assessment of the candidates to the boss.

—The first one is rather vague but has imagination; the second one is educated, determined, but lacks flexibility; the third one is rather stupid, but seems to be improving. Which one would you rather hire?
—The tall blonde one with the long legs.

It would be possible to write an entire treatise on the variations of the "two plus two" joke in eastern European humor. Most of them are less sexist than the version cited above and have to do with the exigencies of politics. A Hungarian text satirizing the Soviet "aid" to Hungary is representative: A master in an elementary school asked his pupils, "Which of you can introduce politics into an arithmetical problem?" One of the children got to his feet and said, "Two and two are four, teacher." "Of course that's right, but there are no politics in that problem." "Two and two are six," volunteered another. "That is not right and, besides, there are no politics in it." Finally little Maurice raises his hand. "Well, let's see what Maurice has to say." "Two and two make three and with the help of the great Soviet Union they make four." "Very good, Maurice." See "Experts in Numbers," *News from Behind the Iron Curtain,* 2, no. 5 (May, 1953): 54. Equally interesting is a skit allegedly broadcast over Radio Budapest on 28 November 1964, consisting of a dialogue between a reporter and a man in the street who has been selected at random:

—Would you please tell me how much is two times two?
—Sure. Four. Two times two is four.
—Quite sure of that?
—I'll bet my life on it.
—Wonderful. Will you please give this to me in writing?
—What?
—That two times two is four. Just put it down on a piece of paper, date it, and sign it.
—Your request is idiotic. Anyway, I don't have a pen.
—Here, take my fountain pen.
—I refuse to handle someone else's pen. I might pick up germs.
—Well, then, I'll go to your apartment in the evening to get your signature.
—I'll throw you out if you do.
—Honestly, now, tell me why you are so reluctant to sign. You just told me you'd bet your life on the fact that two times two is four.
—I will certainly not give it in writing. You might show this paper to someone sometime in the future.
—Well, so what. Two times two is always four, isn't it?
—Look here. I'm a family man. I never engage in politics.

—This isn't politics.

—I don't know about that. But I want to be on the safe side. Nobody should ever blame me for giving you this statement in writing.

—I've got an idea. I'll give you a paper stating that two times two is four, you sign it, then we're quits and you don't risk a thing.

—Quite unnecessary. If you're so keen on it, though, I'll give you a written statement saying that nowadays people in general believe that two times two is four. O.K.?

—No. I want your personal opinion, because I collect courageous statements of individuals.

—Go to hell!

—All right. But let me tell you, I'll tell everybody that you said two times two is four.

—Who cares? I'll deny it anyway.

See "Playing It Safe," *East Europe,* 14, no. 1 (January, 1965): 49. Sometimes the versions are short. For example, the question "Does two and two make four?" is answered by "What did *Pravda* say this morning?" See Paruit, 1978:158. In another version, the question "How much is two and two?" is answered by the successful candidate with "How much do you want it to be?" See Kolasky, 1972:76. For other versions of the joke, see Hirche, 1964:249–50; anon., 1969b:26; Aranyossy, 1971:393–94 (= Paruit, 1978:184–86); Drozdzynski, 1974:122–23, 198; Filip and Steiger, 1977:54; Hirche, 1977:189; Is-nard, 1977:42; Kalina, 1980:81, 108, 191; and Dolgopolova, 1982:30, 72–73. It should be noted that nonpolitical versions of the joke are known in the West. For example, two men advertise for a bookkeeper. Three young ladies appear for the interview which consists of one test question: How much is twelve times twelve? One girl answered 164, another answered 124, and one had the correct answer, 144. The men discuss which girl to hire. One man says, "Perhaps the girl who said 164 would be good for marking up prices. Maybe the girl who said 124 would be O.K. for making up our income tax. What do you think? The other man replies, "Let's take the girl with the big breasts." See *More Over Sexteen* (New York: Grayson, 1953), 18. It is fascinating to compare the capitalistic content of the Western version of a joke with the political concerns of the same joke behind the Iron Curtain.

In Romania, there are four kinds of engineers:
1. Research engineers. They don't do anything, but at least they know something.

2. *Factory engineers. They don't know anything, but at least they do something.*
3. *Government engineers. They don't know anything, and they don't do anything.*
4. *Engineers at the planning committee. They don't know anything, they don't do anything, and they don't let others do anything either.*

There is an international conference on modern ways of digging tunnels.
The American delegate:
—We have two teams on the two sides of the mountain. One of them has a laser beam, the other one a computer which feels the laser beam and guides the digging team through the mountain. As a result, we have a tunnel.
The Chinese delegate:
—This is a waste of good money. In China, we have two teams digging from the two sides of the mountain. Each of them is armed with Mao's booklet and following the party line; the two teams must meet, and then we have a tunnel.
The Romanian delegate:
—I don't understand all this fuss. When we build a tunnel, we too have two teams digging from the two sides of the mountain. There are only two possibilities: either they meet, then we have a tunnel; or they don't, and then we have two tunnels.

For another Romanian version (with American, French, and Romanian teams), see Paruit, 1978:88–89. For a Czech version (with German, American, and Czech participants), see Swoboda, 1969:49. For an Israeli version with just two protagonists (one French and one Israeli engineer), see Dor and Federmann, 1964:300. For another version (with a Russian and someone from the West), see Melor, 1979:42. In a version from the West, a Jewish firm triumphs over English and American competitors. See Henry D. Spalding, *JewishLaffs* (Middle Village, N.Y.: Jonathan David Publishers, 1982), 14–17.

During the Stalinist reign, science and scientists were also subject to Stalin's personal approval. That's how sometimes less than mediocre scientists were turned overnight into pillars of science.

One such biologist was once conducting an experiment on insects. He placed a flea on a sheet of white paper and ordered: jump! The flea jumped indeed. Then he plucked off the flea's legs and ordered again: jump! Of course the flea didn't move.

The conclusion of the experiment, as noted in the biologist's logbook: When the legs of a flea are cut off, the flea becomes deaf.

For other versions, see Wolfe, 1951:13; Winick, 1964:26; Paruit, 1978:95; Melor, 1979:79–80; Kalina, 1980:143. This joke is also widely known in the West as a parody of the scientific method. For a sample American version, see Alan Dundes, "Science in Folklore? Folklore in Science?" *New Scientist* 76 (1977): 775. For another, see Ray Ginger, *Ray Ginger's Jokebook about American History* (New York: New Viewpoints, 1974), 101.

A new Michurinist achievement: crossing bedbugs with fireflies so that people can read at night while saving electricity.

A number of jokes are told about Michurin, a little-known Russian horticulturist who was often mentioned by Lysenko. He created new strains of vegetables by crossing different species. His theory of hybridization endeared him to Stalin who declared him a pillar of science. Among the jokes: he supposedly invented barbed wire by crossing rainworms with hedgehogs, and he supposedly died by breaking his neck when he fell off one of his strawberries. See Beckmann, 1969:78. For other versions, see Kolasky, 1972:110–11; Drozdzynski, 1974:102; Hirche, 1977:133; and Kalina, 1980:143. In one text we learn that the reason he had no children was because he crossed his wife's legs. See Kalina, 1980:144. In another, the answer to the question "Do you know the last thing that Michurin crossed?" is "the arms on the chest." Melor, 1979:80.

It should be noted that there are many jokes making fun of purported great inventions made by Russian scientists. For example, a foreigner visits a Soviet museum. He sees the bust of a man and asks who it is. "That is comrade Smirnov, the inventor." "What did he invent?" "He invented the radio, the telephone, television, and many other things." "And who is that next to him? There stands another bust." "That is comrade Arimov, also an inventor." "And what did he invent?" "Comrad Smirnov." See Drozdzynski, 1974:58. For other texts of this popular joke, see "Origin of the Species," *News from Behind the Iron Curtain,* 4, no. 1 (January, 1955): 42; Kukin, 1962:[68]; Dor and Federmann, 1964:228; Beckman, 1969:73; Schiff, 1969:113; Kolasky, 1972:111; Benton and Loomes, 1976:123–24; Meyer, 1978:50; Paruit, 1978:160; Melor, 1979:82; and Kalina, 1980:142.

In a Hungarian joke about inventors collected by the second author in Budapest in September 1979, an American digs down in the ground and finds a wire. This proved that Americans invented the telephone one thousand years ago. A Russian digs down and finds nothing. This proves that Russians invented the wireless one thousand years ago. A Hungarian digs down and finds excrement. This proves that Hungarians laid the foundations of socialism two thousand years ago.

—Do you know what's the result of a Michurinist crossing between an idiot and a cap?
—No. What?
—A communist leader.

At a policeman training course the examining officer asks:
—What does all policemen have?
—All policemen has the obligation to . . .
—No, you dumbhead, all policemen has a pair of boots. Now let me try another one. What doesn't all policemen has?
—All policemen doesn't have the right to . . .
—No, you stupid. All policemen doesn't has two pairs of boots. Now I'll asks you a very simple question; you must answer this one: What sleeps in a stable, neighs, has a thick tail, and can gallop very fast?
—I know. Three pairs of boots.

Policemen are a perennial target for jokes. In Romanian the word translates as "militzian" (militiaman), and the saying goes that a "tzian" is a unit of stupidity, but since this is too large for humans, one takes 1/1000 of it, making the *mili*tzian an adequate unit for human stupidity. As in any area of activity, loyalty to the party is the most important criterion for promotion. Accordingly, a police officer need not have any superior merit or intelligence. The "incorrect" form of verbs in the above joke occurs in the Romanian original and is obviously intended to suggest the speech patterns of poorly educated policemen.

—Why do policemen always go around in groups of three?
—One of them can read, another one can write, and the third one keeps a close watch on the two dangerous intellectuals.

In a variant reported from Romania, the question is "Why do the police in Romania always go in pairs?" "Because one reads and the other can write." "And why do they sometimes take a wolfhound with them?" "So they can have an intellectual from the party accompany them." See Jacobi, 1965:130. For another Romanian text, see Brunvand, 1973:188. For Polish versions, see Filip and Steiger, 1977:53; Beckmann, 1980:82; and Kalina, 1980:70. For a Russian version, see Draitser, 1978:49. For additional versions, see Durocher, 1965:71; Benton and Loomes, 1976:136; Isnard, 1977:69; and Meyer, 1978:108.

A policeman enters a bookstore and asks for a book.
—What kind of book would you prefer? A serious work or something light?
—Doesn't matter. I don't have to carry it. I have a car.

For another version, see Meyer, 1978:114.

In 1966 after a period in which abortion was both legal and relatively inexpensive, an overnight presidential decree aimed at increasing the birth rate banned abortion as well as any kind of birth control. The following visual joke is most effective when the drawing is done in front of an audience.
I'm drawing a person:

This is the line of the forehead.

I continue with the line of the nose;

Then comes the line of the mouth, then of the chin.

Now comes the line of the neck,

And this is the line of the Party:

—*Did you hear Ionescu was found dead at the wheel?*
—*What happened? A car crash?*
—*No, there was no car crash. The autopsy didn't reveal any contusion either. All they found were some traces of yogurt in his stomach.*

This joke is probably unintelligible to most Western readers. It has to do with the high cost of automobiles. The French company Renault built a car factory in Romania. Although the cars produced are very small even by European standards and have none of the features of a modern American car (power steering, air conditioning, etc.), their purchase price is very high, especially with respect to Romanian salaries. Individuals who buy a "Dacia" (the word comes from the ancient name of Romania) have to scrimp on everything which is essentially food. Such individuals may eat only yogurt for days on end since yogurt is one of the cheapest foods available. Even after buying the car, the yogurt diet must continue owing to the high-price of gasoline and especially the cost of spare parts which can most of the time be found only on the black market. Because of the shoddiness of the car's construction, it is in frequent need of repair and part replacement. In the above joke, the ultimate effect of diet economizing is death.

Two friends who have both visited Romania meet in Paris. They talk of one thing and another, and finally the discussion turns to cars.

—I just bought a new car, the latest model Mercedes. It cost me four months' salary.

—Well, you know me, I always was a car buff. I bought myself the latest Jaguar which cost me the equivalent of six months' salary. But tell me, have you heard anything lately of our mutual friend Ionescu?

—He is still in Romania. And he bought himself a car, of a make unknown to me, Dacia, which cost him three years' salary.

—Why, I always knew him to be such a snob!

A construction worker on top of a scaffold on a partially occupied building is seized abruptly by stomach cramps. On the assumption that he is well hidden by the scaffolding, the worker relieves himself right there and uses the only piece of paper available to him. But before he is able to dispose of the paper, it is blown away by a blast of wind. To the worker's dismay, he sees it waft through a window in what happens to be the office of the local Living Space Agency's director.

Hoping that the director might be out of his office, the worker hurries down to recover the paper. As he arrives, panting and apologizing at the office door, the secretary tells him:

—Sorry, you're too late, he's already signed it.

To appreciate this joke fully, one needs to know that in order to meet plan deadlines, buildings are frequently reported as completed even when construction work is still going on at the higher levels, and the so-called finished apartments are barely inhabitable. Eager to lay their hands on new apartments to assign to the thousands of people on the long waiting lists, the officials in charge from the Living Space Agency automatically sign for acceptance. Because of the acute housing short-age and in order to ward off any competition, it is quite common for both individuals and institutions to occupy apartments assigned to them regardless of the condition the apartments may be in.

In a Czech version of this joke, the point turns on the shortage of toilet paper. An individual seeing a piece of toilet paper flying through the air follows it in hot pursuit even to the office of the president. In a vain attempt to obtain it, he is told that he is too late for comrade president has just signed it. The equation of toilet paper with signed bureaucratic decrees is explicit enough. See Kalina, 1980:111–12.

At a factory a worker asks the director for permission to take home daily some sawdust and shavings which would be thrown away in any case. The director signs a pass, but after the worker leaves his office, he becomes suspicious. He rings up the guard on duty and asks him to make a very careful inspection of the sawdust to make sure nothing is hidden in it. When the worker arrives at the gate pushing a wheelbar-row full of scrap, the guard stops him, feels thoroughly through it, but can find nothing. The same thing happens again the next day and then the next, for a whole week. The director gets mad with frustration. He asks the worker to come see him in his office.

—Look here, Ilie, I promise nothing will happen to you. But tell me, what's the game?

—Comrade director, I told you. I need the scrap at home. I never take anything else, you can ask the guard.

—I know, I know, but I'm sure you didn't ask for my signature just for some lousy shavings. I give you my word of honor that nothing will happen to you; you may even go on with it as long as you wish, but I have to know. What are you stealing?

—The wheelbarrows, comrade director.

For a Lithuanian version, see "Free Wheeling Time!" *News from Behind the Iron Curtain*, 2, no. 1 (January, 1953): 57. For a Russian version, see Dor and Federmann, 1964:212–13. In a Czech version, a motivation is offered. The puzzled guard gets the worker drunk who then says: "It's like this. I needed to make a rabbit pen, so we could have more meat. And you know how difficult it is to get wood. So I made it out of the fourteen wheelbarrows . . ." See Beckmann, 1969:100–101. For other versions, see Kukin, 1962:[41]; Winick, 1964:25; Durocher, 1965:162; Swoboda, 1969:37; Benton and Loomes, 1976:103–4; Melor, 1979:44–45; Kalina, 1980:190. For an

American version, see Ray Ginger, *Ray Ginger's Jokebook about American History* (New York: New Viewpoints, 1974), 80. For another American text told about "an immigrant laborer from eastern Europe," see Richard M. Dorson, *Land of the Millrats* (Cambridge: Harvard University Press, 1981), 69, 243.

———

Ceausescu is very dissatisfied with the performance of the Romanian army at maneuvers. He summons the war minister, Ionitza.
—Ionitza, why can't we do something about this army? Take examples from history. You remember that great Russian general, you know, the one with the patch on one eye?
—You mean Suvorov?
—Right. Or that Jew who beat the Arabs, the one-eyed guy, you know.
—Yes, Dayan.
—Yes. You know, Ionitza, what about taking out one of your eyes?

For another Romanian version, see Paruit, 1978: 129–30. In this version, Ceausescu says, "You see what you have to do, Ionitza."

———

At a Romanian ministry a new employee is admonished by his supervisor.
—Comrade, I've seen you loafing for the last three days without doing a damn thing.
The new employee looks at him impassively and says:
—You know what? Go jump in the lake.
The supervisor goes to the department head and complains.
—Send the guy to me, says the angry department head.
The undisciplined clerk arrives nonchalantly.
—Comrade, I hear you are neglecting your duties.
—Know what? Kiss my ass.
Exasperated, the department head asks for the employee's file. The personnel chief storms in with a look of panic.
—Comrade director, what are you doing? Don't you know this new clerk is a close relative of the president?
At this revelation, the supervisor exclaims:
—You know, comrade director, I am going to go jump in the lake. You do whatever you think best.

———

—You know that Stalin City was renamed Braşov, while Stalin's works are now called "brasoave"?

Brasov is a beautiful old Romanian city in the Carpathian Mountains. During the Stalinist years, its name was changed into Stalin City. Of course, everybody, resenting the change, continued to refer to it as Brasov. Soon after Khrushchev had denounced Stalin's crimes, the official name of the city was changed back again to the old one. To understand the joke, one needs to know that a derivative word "brasoave" has the meaning of the American word "baloney."

A discussion between two Romanians in the late 1940s.
—Did you hear a new trade agreement has been signed between Romania and the Soviet Union?
—No, what's it about?
—We give them our wheat and in exchange they take our oil.

For another Romanian text, see "Exchange Policy," *News from Behind the Curtain,* 4, no. 3 (March, 1955):42. In a Polish version, the Poles give the Russians coal and in exchange they take the Poles' meat. See Drozdzynski, 1974:114, and Kalina, 1980:128. For an East German version in which the East Germans send the Soviets their consumable products and in exchange the Soviets take the Germans' machine tools, see Paruit, 1978:143. In another East German version, grain is sent to the Soviet Union and the Russians take sugar for it. See Brandt, 1965:13. For another version in which "We export our coal to Russia and in exchange they take our steel," see Kolasky, 1972:41. For a different Romanian joke with a similar message "What is the basis underlying Soviet-Romanian trade relations? Give me your watch and perhaps I will tell you what time it is," see Drozdzynski, 1974:202.

6
Big Brother

—Why do we say, when speaking about the Soviet Union, "our brother" and not "our friend"?
—Because one can choose one's friends.

For other Romanian versions, see Dor and Federmann, 1964:278, and Benton and Loomes, 1976:117; for Czech versions, see Swoboda, 1969:7; Kolasky, 1972:30; and Filip and Steiger, 1977:33; for Polish versions, see Hirche, 1964:299, and Isnard, 1977:20; for Hungarian versions, see Durocher, 1965:128, and Jacobi, 1965:3, For additional versions, see Streit, 1964:28; Meyer, 1978:105; and Paruit, 1978:139.

Popescu talks with his friend.
—You know what happened to me last night? I came home and found my wife in bed with a Russian officer.
—What did you do?
—I tiptoed out, of course. I was lucky. He didn't see me.

For other Romanian versions, see Drozdzynski, 1974:203; Benton and Loomes, 1976:116–17; Isnard, 1977:24; and Melor, 1979:156. For a Czech version, see Kalina, 1980:220; for an East German version, see Jacobi, 1965:102. For another version, see Durocher, 1965:85. This joke is also known in the West. Legman reports a version from New York City dating from 1940. See G. Legman, *Rationale of the Dirty Joke* (New York: Grove Press, 1968), 736.

In 1970 Romania was hit by heavy floods. The damage from the disaster was devastating, and many countries all over the world of-

*fered assistance. America offered twenty million dollars; various other
countries gathered together another ten million.*

*The Soviet Union offered assistance too, by sending one hundred
thousand brochures entitled:*

"How to Learn to Swim in Twenty-four Hours."

For other Romanian versions, see Kolasky, 1972:43; Drozdzynski,
1974:209; and Melor, 1979:70.

While waiting in a long line for bread, Ionescu grumbles.

*—Now we have a bread shortage too. Imagine that! In Romania! A
country which used to export grain! Of course, the Russians take everything away from us, even our bread.*

*As was to be expected, this remark cost Ionescu three months in jail.
Soon after his release, he stays in line to get some oil for his home
heating furnace. Again he grumbles.*

*—I understand why there was an oil shortage during the war. But
now? Now, in an oil-exporting country, to stand in line for oil! They're
sending all our oil to Russia.*

*This time he is sentenced to one year in jail. And sure enough, after
his release, he again talks too much, this time criticizing the butter
shortage. This being the third time that he has been arrested for the
same offense, he gets the maximum sentence: the death penalty. He is
brought before a firing squad. The officer in command orders "Fire,"
but nothing happens. Ionescu is well and alive. The officer tells him:*

*—This time we only wanted to frighten you. But if it ever happens
again, you may be assured that we won't be kidding anymore.*

Ionescu gets out and runs into his friend Popescu.

*—Can you imagine! They even sent our bullets to Russia. They had
to use blanks!*

For another version, see Paruit, 1978:173–74.

---

*—How are commercial exchanges arranged between socialist coun-
tries?*

*—It's like this, For instance, we in Romania have developed a very
good dye for pottery. The dye is made out of human excrement. We
export the pottery to Poland from which we get in exchange poultry.
We then export the eggs to Bulgaria which sends us pork. From it we*

make ham and bacon which we export to Czechoslovakia which in exchange gives us industrial equipment. We export this equipment to Hungary and get in exchange wheat. We export the wheat to the German Democratic Republic and get in exchange buses. We finally export the buses to the Soviet Union.
 —And what do you get from the Soviet Union?
 —The raw material for our excellent dye.

In one Romanian variant, the Russians send coal from which briquets are made for export. See Drozdzynski, 1974:207. In another, it is the Poles who send the coal from which Romanians fabricate briquets for the Soviet Union. See Hirche, 1964:297. In a Czech text, it is also the Soviet Union which sends clay from which pottery is made. See Benton and Loomes, 1976:126–27. In a Polish version, Russia provides the clay. See Durocher, 1965:18–19. The same holds in an earlier Bulgarian version. See "Brickwork," *News from Behind the Iron Curtain,* 5, no. 5 (May, 1956):28. None of these other versions in print, however, are as earthy as the version reported above.

 —Did you hear about the latest Michurin achievement?
 —What is it?
 —He crossed a giraffe and a cow, and the resulting gicow can graze in Romania and be milked in the Soviet Union.

For an earlier Russian version in which it is a "cowraffe" which can graze in Bulgaria while it is being milked in Moscow, see Wolfe, 1951:13. For another version in which a cow with a long neck produced by Soviet biologist Lysenko to feed in Europe and be milked in the USSR is not named, see Kolasky, 1972:107. For other texts, see Hirche, 1964:270; Durocher, 1965:122; Drozdzynski, 1974:102; Benton and Loomes, 1976:126; Meyer, 1978:105; Paruit, 1978:132; Melor, 1979:78; and Kalina, 1980:143.

 Soon after the war a Russian soldier in Romania stops a shepherd in a field and asks the time. The peasant plants his stick into the ground, looks at the angle of the shadow, and tells the time to within ten minutes. After the Russian checks on the five watches he is wearing on his wrist, he snatches the stick saying:
 —Horosho, davai stick [O.K., gimme the stick].

In order to appreciate this joke, one needs to know about the Russian propensity to appropriate watches from individuals in countries under its sway. There are many jokes and anecdotes about this subject.

Few of those who lived in Europe through World War II and the postwar years can have failed to see the famous Soviet picture showing the raising of the Red flag on the Reichstag in Berlin, a picture as famous as the Mount Suribachi (Iwo Jima) flag raising is for Americans. However, it is only the inhabitants of the countries overrun by the Soviet Army who surely noticed that each of the two Russian soldiers holding the flag had several watches on each of his wrists. (This slip was touched up and concealed in later releases of the picture.)

Wherever they went, Russian troops used to rob people of their watches. For them, watches were a typical sign of Western civilization which at that time were unavailable in Russia. The curt order: "Davai chas," translatable as "gimme your watch" became well known in all countries, whether conquered or allied, through which the Soviet troops had marched.

This is why when a huge statue of Stalin was placed at the entrance of one of Bucharest's principal parks, people nudged one another secretly when they noticed that his outstretched hand was reaching toward a big clock across the square. The statue was popularly referred to as the Davai-chas statue.

For a Czech account of the Russian penchant for confiscating watches, see Beckmann, 1969:82–83. In a text set in Hungary at the time of the Hungarian revolution in 1956, it was suggested that it was not worth the trouble to search for two bulldozers to knock down the statue of Stalin in Budapest. One needed only to place a watch in front of the pedestal, and Stalin would descend all by himself. See Isnard, 1977:90.

A Russian soldier looks at the watch on his wrist and is unpleasantly surprised to discover that it has stopped. He shakes it, holds it to his ear, and shakes it again. An eight-year-old boy passing on the street gestures to him that he wants to have a look at the watch. After winding it, he hands it back to the Russian who is amazed that the watch works again. He asks, in wonder:
—*Are you an engineer?*

For a version set in Hungary, see Paruit, 1978:136.

Brezhnev, accompanied by his wife, is on his way back home from an
official visit to Bulgaria. They travel by train, and the trip seems long to
Mrs. Brezhnev who keeps asking her husband how far they still are
from Moscow. Each time, Brezhnev sticks his hand out of the window
before answering, The first time, somebody kisses his hand, so he an-
swers:
—We are still in Bulgaria.
The second time, somebody spits on his hand, and he answers:
—Now we are in Romania.
The third time, he answers:
—Now we are finally in Russia.
—How do you know?
—Somebody stole my wristwatch.

For another Romanian version, see Brunvand, 1973:188. For other
versions, see Brandt, 1965:142; Kolasky, 1972:78; Benton and
Loomes, 1976:124–25; Paruit, 1978:136; and Kalina, 1980:51–52. In a
Russian version, Khrushchev and Bulganin are travelling. It is night
and the radio is not working. They don't know where they are.
Khrushchev tells Bulganin to put his hand out the window. He does so
and it is kissed. Bulganin is next instructed to put his leg out. It too is
kissed. Then Khrushchev orders Bulganin to hold his backside out the
window. It is likewise kissed. Then Khrushchev explains, "Now I
know where we are—in Czechoslovakia!" See Drozdzynski, 1974:80,
and Melor, 1979:69. In a variant text, the question posed is: how can
one orient oneself at night? The answer is with a watch. One takes it in
one's hand, and the direction in which it disappears is east! See Isnard,
1977:90.

The following discussion takes place between Brezhnev and Kosygin
after a Warsaw Pact meeting:
—Did you see the beautiful watch Nixon gave Ceausescu?
—No. Show it to me.

For a Polish version (with the same two discussants but the watch in
question given to Gierek by Pompidou), see Drozdzynski, 1974:147.
For another version (with the same discussants but the watch given to
Ceausescu by de Gaulle), see Benton and Loomes, 1976:97. For a
Hungarian version in which Szabó takes the watch of American mil-
lionaire Cyrus Eaton, see Jacobi, 1965:9. In a somewhat older version
the owner of the watch is Poland's Gomulka. See Larsen, 1980:91.

Larsen also cites a text (1980:14) which he claims was current in 1815; Three soldiers of the Allied armies, a Prussian, an Austrian, and a Russian, happen to share the same quarters. When they are marching the next day, the Prussian says, "Did you see the beautiful little clock on the mantelpiece? I wanted to put it in my knapsack, but that was already full." "Wait a minute, mates, I'll go back and get it," says the Austrian. "No use," says the Russian. "I've got it already." This would make the Russian's alleged penchant for stealing clocks and watches quite a long-standing tradition.

A Romanian and a Russian are taking a stroll through a field. Suddenly they see a suitcase on the ground. They open it and behold! It is full of banknotes. The Russian looks around to make sure they're not being watched. Then he says:
—We'll share this fraternally.
—Sorry, says the Romanian, this time we'll make it fifty-fifty.

For other versions, see Meyer, 1978:99; Melor, 1979:61; Beckmann, 1980:66; and Kalina, 1980:218.

An indoctrination class in the mid 1960s at a Romanian collective farm.
—The Soviets are winning the space race and will soon fly to the moon, says the lecturer.
—All of them? asks a peasant hopefully.

For another Romanian version, see Benton and Loomes, 1976:117. For Czech versions, see "Current Humor in Czechoslovakia," *East Europe,* 18, nos. 11–12 (November–December, 1969): 52; Kolasky, 1972:30; Larsen, 1980:85. For Polish versions, see Langnas, 1963:20; and Drozdzynski, 1974:139; for East German versions, see Dor and Federmann, 1964:147, and Brandt, 1965:160; for a Hungarian version, see Jacobi, 1965:8. For additional versions, see Durocher, 1965:122; Paruit, 1978:127; and Melor, 1979:72.

—What do the Soviet Union and the Garden of Eden have in common?
—?!?!?

—On getting out of the Soviet Union, every couple is like Adam and Eve leaving the Garden of Eden: naked and knowing.

—Stalin dies and goes to hell. There he meets the last czar who asks him:
    —What has become of my beloved Russia?
    —Stronger and greater than ever.
    —What about my secret police?
    —As strong as ever.
    —And the Siberian camps?
    —They continue to exist and are as good a deterrent as ever.
    —What about the vodka? Still thirty-eight proof?
    —Better. We now make it forty proof.
    —What! Do you mean to tell me that two lousy degrees were worth all that upheaval?

For other versions, see Beckmann, 1969:29; Swoboda, 1969:44; Benton and Loomes, 1976:153; Paruit, 1978:95–96; Melor, 1979:11–12; Larsen, 1980:85–86; and Kalina, 1980:83–84.

A dog is launched in an early Russian space vehicle, and as it orbits the earth, the dog receives invitations from all of the nations of the world to descend.
    —Come land in our country, urge the French and Italians.
    —No, replies the dog, I must return to Moscow.
    —Why?
    —Because Moscow is the best place in the world to lead the life of a dog.

Other jokes play on space flights. For example, the first Russian to reach Venus returns to earth. Khrushchev asks him if life is possible on Venus. He answers, "No, not there either." See Dor and Federmann, 1964:242; Brandt, 1965:253; and Kalina, 1980:226. In another version, the question is posed to a returning cosmonaut: "Is there life in space?" His answer: "There is no life there either." See Kolasky, 1972:98. For the same joke on the moon, see Kalbouss 1977:449. In a variant, a Czech boy asks his father, "Is it true that the Russians have landed on the moon?" "Yes, it's true." "And it is true that people can live on the moon?" "Not any more." See Benton and Loomes, 1976:112.

Question for Radio Erevan.
—*Why do we punish our saboteurs by exiling them to Siberia which is still part of our socialist paradise instead of exiling them to the capitalist hell of the West and getting rid of them?*
—*Because we couldn't afford the sudden increase of millions of saboteurs.*

For other versions, see Schiff, 1969:47; Kolasky, 1972:120; and Melor, 1979:218.

Question for Radio Erevan.
—*Is it possible for a dog to have a nervous breakdown?*
—*Yes, it is possible, but only if the dog leads the life of a man.*

For another version in which the question addressed to Radio Erevan is whether a dog in the USSR can get a heart attack with the answer: "Yes, if he is forced to live like a human," see Kolasky, 1972:98. In another text the answer is, "Yes, if one compels him to live under the same conditions in which the citizens of socialist countries live." Durocher, 1965:72.

Ivan, desperate because he cannot make ends meet while most of his fellow workers are doing quite well on the same salary, decided to go and see Stalin, his old school-days crony, and get some help or advice from him. He is received at the Kremlin by the first secretary. After listening to him, Stalin asks Ivan:
—*At what time do you arrive at the plant in the morning?*
—*At 7:00 like everybody else.*
—*Try to be there at 6:30 and come see me in a month.*
The advice is followed. Ivan is amazed to see that at 6:30 there is quite a commotion in the factory yard. People are moving hurriedly, their pockets bulging as they get out through the gates. A worker sees him and surreptitiously slips a ten ruble note in his hand. At 7:00 all is quiet again, and workers are pouring in through the gates. He tries it again next day, and again for a whole week. Life conditions begin to improve for him. After a week he decides to try an even earlier hour. He gets to the factory at 6 A.M. At that time busy workers are rushing out the gates, loaded with heavy packs. Someone slips a twenty ruble bill into his hand. Next day, he gets to the factory at 5:00 in the morning. Heavy trucks loaded with crates are leaving the plant. He looks at the

guards and one of them quickly slips a one hundred ruble bill into his hand.

At the end of the month, he is again received by Stalin.

—How are things going now, Ivan?

—Fine, although I'm a bit tired. There's only one thing I don't under-stand (looking at the luxury around him). When, comrade Stalin, do you manage to sleep?

Question for Radio Erevan.

—How come the Armenian Republic has a Ministry of the Navy even though it has no outlet to the sea?

—It's not so unusual. Don't they have a Ministry of Culture in the Georgian Republic?

For Czech versions, see Swoboda, 1969:57; Drozdzynski, 1974:162; Filip and Steiger, 1977:42; and Dolgopolova, 1982:37–38. In yet another Czech version, the surprise that Czechoslovakia, a country which does not border on the sea, is going to have an Admiralty is answered by "So what, we have a Justice Department, don't we?" See Beckmann, 1969:16. For other versions, see Brandt, 1965:153, and Paruit, 1978:35. For versions set in Nazi Germany, see Gamm, 1979[1963]:13; and Larsen, 1980:51.

Question for Radio Erevan.

—Is it true that in the Soviet Union people do not need stereophonic equipment?

—In principle, yes. One hears exactly the same thing from all sides anyway.

For other versions, see Schiff, 1969:16; Kolasky, 1972:120; Benton and Loomes, 1976:142; Melor, 1979:104; and Kalina, 1980: 174.

Teacher:

—What pictures do you have on your walls at home, children?

Dmitri:

—We have a portrait of Lenin.

Ivan:

—We have a reproduction of Repin's.

Teacher:

—Good! And you, Sasha?
—Comrade teacher, we have no picture since we have no walls.
—What do you mean?
—We are living in the middle of the room.

There was a time when the housing shortage in the big cities of the Soviet Union was so acute that several families shared not just one apartment, but just one room. In an earlier Russian version, the punch line is: "Please, teacher, the other four families have the walls; we live in the center of the room." See Wolfe, 1951:13. For another Russian version, see Winick, 1964:56.

After Khrushchev's visit to the United States, he decided that in order to attract American visitors to the Soviet Union he should start a striptease show in one of the nightclubs set up for tourists. The manager must obey strict party guidelines in selecting the performer. The candidates are screened on the basis of political grounds: social origin, loyalty to the party, political reliability.

Khrushchev attends the opening show. A heavy woman wearing a long peasant skirt and heavy boots appears on the scene and begins clumsily to undress. Under her skirt, a yellowish underskirt of rough fabric appears, its length just uncovering the flat boots and woollen stockings.

Khrushchev's aide comments:
—I'm damned if I can understand what these capitalists find so exciting about striptease!

For a German text in which Radio Erevan explains that all the dancers must have been good party members for at least forty years, see Parth and Schiff, 1972:15. In other versions, the dancers must have been at least thirty years in the party (Benton and Loomes, 1976:82), twenty years in the party (Kolasky, 1972:54), or participants in the October Revolution (of 1917) (Drozdzynski, 1974:91; Filip and Steiger, 1977:14; Paruit, 1978:72; Kalina, 1980:47; Larsen, 1980:83–84; and Dolgopolova, 1982:107).

A Russian and an American have an argument over where life is better: in America or in Russia. The Russian speaks:
—Things are permanently improving in our country. Now I have a two-room apartment for me and my family of four. I'm satisfied with

my housing conditions, so I can't complain. I still stand in line for certain food staples like meat and fresh vegetables, but I can buy bread without queuing, so I can't complain. Even public transportation has improved considerably. In the morning I seldom wait more than a half hour before being able to board a bus to take me to my office, and I seldom have to hang on to bars at the bus entrance steps, so I can't complain.

The American speaks:

I, too, am satisfied with my four bedroom house for my family of four. I find any food item I wish, including meat and fresh vegetables, at the supermarket, and I shop only once or twice a week without ever standing in line. I drive to the office in my own car, and the only trouble I have is traffic jams. And moreover, I can complain.

It should be noted that unlike the American two-bedroom apartment in which at least a living room if not also a dining room is taken for granted, an eastern European two-room apartment means two rooms. Period. For Polish versions of this joke, see "The Right Department," *East Europe*, 8, no. 4 (April, 1959): 34; and Drozdzynski, 1974:119. For other versions, see Durocher, 1965:57–58; Swoboda, 1969:16; Kolasky, 1972:124; Benton and Loomes, 1976:139–40; Isnard, 1977:18; Melor, 1979:65–66; and Larsen, 1980:96.

An American and a Russian get into an argument over which of their peoples is happier. They decide that each should give a description of a typical workday. The American begins:

—I get up at 7:00, I have breakfast, then I drive to my office. I work from 8:30 to 5:00, with a half-hour break for lunch. Then I drive back to my suburban house. I have dinner and spend most evenings of the week with my family, watching TV in the family room. If the children are not interested, they can retire each to his own room, or they may watch another program on a second TV set. I think this is a happy life.

The Russian speaks:

—I get up at 5:30, I have breakfast, then I go to work. On my way, I stop at a shop to stand in line for bread. Then I wait for a bus to take me to my office. If I'm lucky, I don't wait more than half an hour, and I don't have to hang on the bus stairboard. I work from 8:30 to 4:30, have lunch, and then, if there isn't any political meeting, I put in two hours of "voluntary labor" out of my assigned ten hours per week. This way I'll have my Sunday off to spend with my family. I leave at 7:00, stop on my way at different shops to see if they have any choice items.

If they do, I stand in line. When I get home, I'm so tired after dinner I go right to bed and fall asleep in a minute. At 2:00 in the morning, I hear a bang on my door. I'm panic-stricken. I reach for my bundle, always at hand. Then I hear a voice asking:

—Does comrade Ivanov live here?

—No, I answer. He lives next door.

The relief of knowing they're looking for Ivanov, not for me! The happiness of it! This is a kind of happiness you Americans are deprived of.

In this and the preceding joke there is a reference to rush hour traffic during which people hang like grapes on the stairboards/entrance steps of buses and electric cars. For Czech versions of this joke, see "We Live More Joyfully," *News from Behind the Iron Curtain*, 1, no. 1 (January, 1952): 28; Beckmann, 1969:19; and anon., 1977:850. For other texts, see Drozdzynski, 1974:48; Meyer, 1978:119; Paruit, 1978:34; and Melor, 1979:143.

At an international conference in New York all hotel rooms are booked so that latecomers have to share rooms. That is how an Englishman happened to share a room with a Russian on the twenty-fifth floor of a hotel. One night the Russian jumps out of the window and kills himself. Of course, the first to be interrogated is the Englishman who gives the following account:

—Well, we got along very well, only each of us was used to living according to his habits. When I got home in the evening, I sat comfortably in an armchair and started reading the Times *because that's what we are used to doing. He opened a bottle of vodka and started drinking because that's what they are used to doing. Then I went to the bathroom to take a bath because that's what we are used to doing. He stretched out on the bed with his boots on because that is what they are used to doing. Then I put on my pajamas, went to bed, and turned off the night-table light because that is what we are used to doing. He took off his pants and shirt and fell asleep with his light on because that is what they are used to doing. Last night, towards midnight, somebody knocked at our door. I woke up, put on a robe, and went to see who it was because that is what we are used to doing. He rushed to the window and jumped out because that is what they are used to doing.*

For other versions, see Swoboda, 1969:23; Paruit, 1978:29–30; and Kalina, 1980:63.

An American delegation touring the USSR is shown around a modern factory. In front of it there is a huge vacant lot with just one car parked in it. An American asks:
—*Who does this factory belong to?*
—*To the workers, of course.*
—*And the car?*
—*To its director.*
At the same time, a Soviet delegation is touring the United States. They also visit a factory. In front of it is a huge parking lot crammed with cars. A Russian asks:
—*Who does this factory belong to?*
—*To its owner, Mr. Smith.*
—*And all these cars?*
—*To the workers, of course.*

For other versions, see Kolasky, 1972:63; Drozdzynski, 1974:97; Paruit, 1978:64, 187–88; Melor, 1979:152; and Kalina, 1980:230.

Khrushchev and Eisenhower were once discussing living standards in their respective countries. Khrushchev asks Eisenhower:
—*How much does an average American worker earn per month?*
—*Three hundred dollars a month.*
—*And how much does he need to meet basic requirements?*
—*Two hundred and fifty dollars a month.*
—*And what does he do with the difference?*
—*That's his business.*
Now it's Khrushchev's turn to answer.
—*How much does an average Soviet worker make a month?*
—*Eight hundred rubles a month.*
—*And how much does he need to meet basic requirements?*
—*One thousand one hundred rubles a month.*
—*And how does he get the difference?*
—*That's his business.*

In order to understand this joke, one must bear in mind that moonlighting is illegal in communist countries where supposedly salaries are high, since these are workers' states, and the factories as well as all means of production "belong to the people." In practice, salaries are so low that the average worker lives under conditions that in America would be considered below the poverty level unless the worker is able to supplement his salary by stealing on the job whatever isn't nailed down.

For an earlier Romanian version of this joke, see "Laissez Faire," *News from Behind the Iron Curtain*, 1, no. 7 (July, 1952): 47. For a Polish version, see "Economic Semantics," *News from Behind the Iron Curtain*, 5, no. 9 (September, 1956): 30. For a Hungarian version, see "Jokes from Hungary," *East Europe*, 13, no. 10 (October, 1964): 47. For Czech versions, see Swoboda, 1969:15, and Beckmann, 1980:98. For versions set in Yugoslavia, see Lewis, 1956:12; Dor and Federmann, 1964:292; and Meyer, 1978:77. For other versions, see Winick, 1964:54; Durocher, 1965:22–23; Drozdzynski, 1974:96; Isnard, 1977:13; and Melor, 1979:54.

Dialogue between two Soviet writers:
—What are you working on now?
—I'm writing about a young man in Moscow . . .
—I see, a story.
—. . . he meets a young girl and they fall in love . . .
—Ah, a love story.
—. . . they get married and find an apartment in Moscow . . .
—Ah, a fairy tale.

For other versions, see Drozdzynski, 1974:46, and Melor, 1979:30.

An American jet is on the point of landing at Moscow airport. The stewardess announces:
—We are now landing in the Soviet Union. Please tighten your belts!
—A Russian who happens to be on the jet says angrily:
—No politics, please!

For a Russian version in which a Soviet plane lands in Peking, see Bregman, 1967:22. For another version in which a French plane with a Soviet journalist aboard lands at the Moscow airport, see Paruit, 1978:109. The joke is reminiscent of a text set at a mass meeting in a Polish steelworks. The speaker says, "We must tighten our belts!" From the back of the crowd, a voice asks, "Where do we get the belts from?" See Benton and Loomes, 1976:102. In another version placed in 1960, Mao Tse-tung cabled to Khrushchev, "Starving. Send grain." Khrushchev replied, "Short of grain ourselves. Can't send any. Tighten your belts." Whereupon Mao Tse-tung responded, "Send belts." See Parry, 1966:14. For other versions, see Winick, 1964:32; Draitser, 1978:39; and Melor, 1979:104.

The Russians are extremely proud of their Moscow subway, the
Metro, with its stations decorated out of proportion. Every visitor in
Moscow is taken through it.
An American tourist is guided through a metro station. On the track
platform the guide says:
—On each of these tracks a train runs every three minutes.
—But we've been here for almost half an hour, and I saw no train on
either track.
—You should talk! You Americans, who beat the Negroes!

For an early version, see Dallin, 1949:15. For other versions of this
popular joke, see Dor and Federmann, 1964:225; Hirche, 1964:288;
Durocher, 1965:70; Beckmann, 1969:84; Schiff, 1969:103; Swoboda,
1969:14; anon., 1971:22; Drozdzynski, 1974:62; Filip and Steiger,
1977:40; Meyer, 1978:60–61; Paruit, 1978:169; and Kalina, 1980:250.

During the Great Depression two unemployed American workers
decide to try their luck in the Soviet Union. But since so many con-
tradictory rumors are circulating about this workers' paradise and so
little reliable information is available, they determine to act cautiously.
Jack will go first, see things with his own eyes, and if everything's all
right, he will write to Bill urging him to follow.
—But what if they have censorship?
—Look, here's what I'll do. I'll write only good things. If my letter is
written in blue ink, everything I write is true. If it's in red ink, then the
reverse of what I write is true.
Three months after Jack's departure, Bill gets a letter from him. He
opens it and to his great relief, he sees that the ink is blue. Then he
reads the letter:
"Dear Bill, everything here is wonderful. There is no unemployment,
wages are high and increasing steadily, there's plenty of food and of
clothing, everybody lives in large, beautiful apartments. This is a para-
dise for working-people. There's freedom and there's plenty. There's
only one thing I couldn't find: red ink.

In most versions of this joke it is green ink which is lacking. So it is in
a version from the Nazi era, told as part of the popular Cologne fool
cycle of stories centering on the characters Tünnes and Schäl. See
Hirche, 1964:167. For other green ink texts, see Kukin, 1962:[32];
Aranyossy, 1971:331; Drozdzynski, 1974:38–39; Benton and Loomes,
1976:132–33; Isnard, 1977:99–100; Paruit, 1978:188–89; and Melor,
1979:216–17. There are, however, versions with no red ink. See

Swearingen, 1961:4; Winick, 1964:36; Durocher, 1965:145–46; Beck-mann, 1969:66; Kolasky, 1972:92; and Meyer, 1978:74. The metaphor-ical irony is perhaps more piquant with *red* ink!

There are other jokes based upon "secret" coded messages. For example, Krushchev, upon his return from the United States, says to Mikoyan, "The Jews of America are powerful, and they are making propaganda against us. It is necessary to prove to them that we are not anti-Semitic. Let us convoke the synod of all the rabbis of the Soviet Union and compel them to declare that they are free and well-treated here." The great synod is convoked, at the end of which the rabbis drew up a statement addressed to American Jews: "Soviet Judaism is well. The Jews are content with their lot, and they lack nothing except sugar and candles." Krushchev reads the statement and asks, "Why do you ask for sugar and candles?" "So that they will believe us. If we say that we lack nothing, they won't believe us." Krushchev approves the statement which is sent to the United States. In America Jewish lead-ers ponder the content of the statement, and finally a Talmudic scholar discovers its true meaning. "If they say to us to send them sugar, this proves that they live in bitterness; and if they ask us to send them candles, this proves that they live in darkness." See Durocher, 1965:141–42. For other representative texts, see Winick, 1964:6–7; and Melor, 1979:204–5.

Stalin has died, but neither heaven nor hell wanted to accept him. While waiting outside the gates of hell, Stalin sees an old crony of his, an athlete, come by. Seeing Stalin's dejection at being kept out, he tries to help him. He asks Stalin to get into a large bag. Then hoisting it on his shoulders, Stalin's old friend knocks at the gates. A devil appears. The friend asks:
—Do you have here a man by the name of Karl Marx?
—Yes, we have.
—Well, I brought the interest on his Capital.

For an earlier version of this joke, see Kukin, 1962:[17]. For other versions, see Hirche, 1964:284; Brandt, 1965:132–33; Beckmann, 1969:28; Kolasky, 1972:5; Drozdzynski, 1974:75; Melor, 1979:125–126; and Larsen, 1980:82.

A few days after Stalin's admission to hell, there's a great commo-tion at the gates of heaven: the devils are asking for political asylum.

For East German versions about Ulbricht, see Hirche, 1964:224; Streit, 1964:28; Brandt, 1965:230–31; Jacobi, 1965:107; and Drozd-zynski, 1974:175. For other versions, see Kukin, 1962:[34]; Hirche, 1964:284; Winick, 1964:5; Kolasky, 1972:6; Benton and Loomes, 1976:152; Isnard, 1977:98; and Kalina, 1980:239.

This joke is almost certainly a modern version of a standard European folktale in which a shrewish woman goes to hell causing the devil to flee. See tale type 1164, "The Evil Woman Thrown into the Pit," in Antti Aarne and Stith Thompson, *The Types of the Folktale* (Helsinki, 1961). The same plot is the basis for a ballad. See Child Ballad #278, "The Farmer's Curst Wife," in Francis James Child, *The English and Scottish Popular Ballads,* vol. 5 (New York, 1962). For representative scholarship, see Stanislaus Prato, "Vergleichende Mitteilungen zu Hans Sachs Fastnachtspiel Der Teufel mit dem alten Weib," *Zeitschrift für Volkskunde* 9 (1899): 189–94, 311–21; V. Bugiel, "La Femme Pire que le Diable," *Revue des Traditions Populaires* 28 (1913): 145–52, 217–24, 293–305; and Ellen J. Stekert, "The Farmer's Curst Wife—A Modified Historic-Geographic Study" (M.A. in folklore thesis, Indiana University, 1961), 136 pp.

A Russian economist, on official business in New York City, wants to make a trip through the states. He calls the State Department:
—I'd like a visa to go to Niagara Falls.
—The Canadian side?
—No, the American side.
—Then you don't need any visa.
—You mean I can travel in the direction of the border without a special permit?
—Certainly. Americans can even cross the Canadian border without a visa.
—Well, I'll be damned! Now I have another problem. I want to buy a car in time to make the trip before I leave the country. What should I do?
—Do you have the money?
—Yes.
—Then what's the problem? Go and buy your car.
—You mean I can go ahead of the waiting list?
—No, we don't have waiting lists in America.
—And how do I get ration tickets for gasoline?
—We don't have ration tickets in America. You can buy any amount of gas you want at any gas station.

—Even outside New York?
—Anywhere in America.
The Russian hangs up, muttering:
—Well, that's America. What anarchy!

For another Romanian text, see Brunvand, 1973:182. For other versions, see Dor and Federmann, 1964:210; Hirche, 1964:289; Durocher, 1965:54–55; Beckmann, 1969:85; Drozdzynski, 1974:42–43; Isnard, 1977:89; and Davies, 1981:155. This joke shows how hard it is for members of one culture to understand another culture. Americans, for example, have trouble comprehending the communist way of life. Their first reaction upon hearing accounts of life under communism is one of disbelief. Some even consider what they're told as malicious, slanderous propaganda. In trying to understand the communist way of life, Americans apply to it their own standards, and as a result, the picture they perceive is greatly distorted. The same holds true in reverse. When one tries to explain to a Russian what American life is like, he listens in disbelief, thinking what he hears is only capitalist propaganda. When he realizes that the person speaking to him really means what he says, the Russian considers such a person as hopelessly naive and gullible. When Russians come to the United States, they naturally enough tend to apply their own standards to life around them. This interpretation or rather misinterpretation of American life is well illustrated in the above joke.

A Soviet politician is in America for the first time. He speaks to his American counterpart:
—Your economy is in terrible shape.
—What do you mean? Don't you think our shops are well stocked?
—Oh, certainly, but most people are too poor to buy anything. If a single item you have here on display were to be imported into the Soviet Union, it would sell in a few hours, and the queue would be one mile long. I've been here for two weeks, and I haven't yet seen a single queue.

For another version told about Molotov going to Berlin on a diplomatic mission in 1939, see Kolasky, 1972:88. For another version set in West Germany, see Benton and Loomes, 1976:98. For a version in which a Soviet journalist visits Denmark, see Paruit, 1978:163. For other versions set in western Europe, see Durocher, 1965:18; Meyer, 1978:73; Beckmann, 1980:72; and Davies, 1981:153.

In 1946, a Russian official returning from a trip to America is asked about his impressions.

—The Americans are a very backward people. I traveled a lot by train, and I didn't see a single delousing station.

Churchill, Roosevelt, and Stalin meet in heaven, and they start discussing their relative importance.

—I was the most important, says Churchill, since I was the master of the waters which God created at the beginning of the world.

—I was more important, says Roosevelt, since I was the master of the air [heaven] which existed before the waters.

—You're both wrong, says Stalin. According to The Creation, in the beginning there was chaos. And I was the master of chaos.

In a Hungarian text, a lawyer, doctor, architect, and fanatic Communist sit in a small restaurant in Budapest arguing about whose profession is the oldest. "First there was a judge," declared the lawyer, "for without laws the first men could not have known how to exist." "Nonsense," countered the doctor, "We know that Cain and Abel were born, and how could this have happened without any obstetrician?" The architect laughed loudly, "Long before this there must have been an architect who created order out of the chaotic world." "Aha," cried the Communist, "and who created chaos?" See Hirche, 1964:292.

One of the great achievements of communism is to have proven the Bible wrong. According to the Bible, in the beginning there was chaos, and then there was order.

The Russians know that first there was planning, and then there was chaos.

For another version, see Kolasky, 1972:129.

A Russian and an American discuss what freedom means in their respective countries.

—I can go to the White House, says the American, and shout: "The president of the United States is an idiot" and nothing will happen to me.

—Big deal! says the Russian. I, too, can go to the Kremlin and shout: "The president of the United States is an idiot" and nothing will happen to me, either.

For an earlier Russian version, see Dallin, 1949:15. For other versions of this widespread joke, see Swearingen, 1961:5; Kukin, 1962:[81]; Dor and Federmann, 1964:229; Durocher, 1965:58; Swoboda, 1969:8–9; Kolasky, 1972:123; Parth and Schiff, 1972:105; Drozdzynski, 1974:88; Isnard, 1977:17–18; Meyer, 1978:118; Paruit, 1978:81; Melor, 1979:54; Kalina, 1980:127; and Dolgopolova, 1982:32.

There are other jokes which play upon an alleged "similarity" between life behind the Iron Curtain and life in the United States. For example, "How is it alike in Poland and the United States?" "Here, as there, one cannot buy anything with zlotys." Kalina, 1980:131, and Davies, 1981:154. Incidentally, jokes about the weakness of the local currency are not uncommon. In one text, at a conference of Polish economists devoted to how to raise the value of the zloty, one economist proposed drilling four holes in them and selling them as buttons. See Kolasky, 1972:37. In another text, "Did you hear the latest? Tito has been nominated for the Nobel Prize in chemistry?" "No, what for?" "He succeeded in making dung out of dinars!" Jacobi, 1965:141.

Khrushchev once made a trip to England. Before going to Buckingham Palace to see the queen, he was told that protocol demanded that he kiss the queen's hand. This humiliation before a monarch was more than he as a communist chief of state could bear. Not knowing how to get out of this difficulty, he conjured up Lenin's ghost and asked for advice.

—Oh, stop making all that fuss about kissing a lady's hand, came Lenin's answer, you who for thirty years have done nothing but kiss Stalin's ass!

For a Czech version, see Beckmann, 1969:42.

Brezhnev speaks to the Central Committee:
—Comrades, after successful completion of our five-year plan, we'll have built the communist society, and we will thus be able to prove to the whole world the basic superiority of communism over capitalism. We will then extend our influence over the entirety of Europe as well as over the third world, and, if necessary, we will conquer them.
Kosygin asks him:
—Why not also conquer the United States and include them, too, in the communist world?

—Are you crazy? says Brezhnev, where then are we going to get our wheat from?

This is hardly a joke considering that the socialist countries are indeed very dependent upon the capitalist world for both food and technology. For other texts of this joke, see "Consolation," *East Europe,* 6, no. 2 (February, 1957): 56; Winick, 1964:50; Durocher, 1965:26; Jacobi, 1965:81; Parry, 1966:14; Kolasky, 1972:15; Drozdzynski, 1974:67; Draitser, 1978:47; Meyer, 1978:56; Melor, 1979:38; and Kalina, 1980:230.

Question for Radio Erevan.
—How come Canada and the United States can sell us so much wheat?
—The fault lies with the catastrophic capitalist overproduction.

For other versions, see Hirche, 1964:294; Brandt, 1965:152; Jacobi, 1965:75; Schiff, 1969:100; Melor, 1979:50; Kalina, 1980:207; and Davies, 1981:154.

—What is the greatest achievement of Soviet agriculture?
—To sow wheat in the Soviet Union and to harvest it in America.

A Hungarian version of this joke goes as follows: Why did Khrushchev get a Nobel Prize last year? For having sown wheat in Siberia and harvested it in Canada. See "Jokes from Hungary," *East Europe,* 13, no. 10 (October, 1964): 47. For other texts, see Hirche, 1964:290; Streit, 1964:28; Sulzberger, 1964:26; Durocher, 1965:69–70; Kolasky, 1972:11, 108; Drozdzynski, 1974:78; Hirche, 1973:131; Meyer, 1978:19, 46; Paruit, 1978:100; Melor, 1979:34; and Kalina, 1980:144.

Another harvest political joke turns on a Russian boast that Russians harvest four times a year: first in Russia, then in Poland, then in Czechoslovakia, and finally in Hungary. For a version from Yugoslavia, see "As ye sow . . ." *News from Behind the Iron Curtain,* 1, no. 2 (February, 1952): 42; for a Czech version, see "Jokes Current in East Europe," *East Europe,* 17, no. 3 (March, 1968): 49. For other versions, see Hirche, 1964:270; Parth and Schiff, 1972:48; Benton and Loomes, 1976:125; Steiger, 1976:73; Paruit, 1978:139; and Melor, 1979:59.

There is a dispute between different nations concerning the origin of Adam and Eve with particular regard to their probable nationality.

The Englishman argues:

—They must have been English because only an Englishman would be so much a gentleman as to give his twelfth rib to make a woman.

The Frenchman contends:

—They were French because only a Frenchman could be so elegant while completely naked.

The Jew insists:

—They must have been Jews because the Bible says the creation took place in the Holy Land.

—Finally, the Romanian claims:

—They must have been Russian because only Russians could share one measly apple, be dressed so poorly, and still call it Paradise.

Few jokes are more popular than this one. For other versions, see Wolfe, 1951:13; Kukin, 1962:[67]; Hirche, 1964:228, 286; Winick, 1964:17; Brandt, 1965:79; Durocher, 1965:121; Swoboda, 1969:36; Mikes, 1971:145; Kolasky, 1972:99; Drozdzynski, 1974: 94; Michael, 1974:32; Benton and Loomes, 1976:141; anon., 1977:940; Hirche, 1977:94; Isnard, 1977:16; Meyer, 1978:67; Paruit, 1978:158; Melor, 1979:218; Beckmann, 1980:63; Kalina, 1980:80; Larsen, 1980:82; and Dolgopolova, 1982:53.

Question for Radio Erevan.

—Is it true that in the Soviet Union we don't need censorship of the mail?

—In principle, yes. Letters with anti-Soviet content are not forwarded, anyway.

For other versions, see Kolasky, 1972:120; Parth and Schiff, 1972:54; and Drozdzynski, 1974:70.

—Will the Soviet rockets win the moon race?

—In principle, yes. For we've got the better Germans.

For another version of this obviously dated joke, see Schiff, 1969:115. In an East German text, the Russian Sputnik and the American Explorer encounter one another in space. The Russian vehicle expresses a greeting in Russian; the American answers in English, but then proposes, "Let's stop this nonsense and speak German with one another. No one can hear us here." See Brandt, 1965:155, who also observes that this "robot fable" is a logical development of the older animal fable.

—*What is the definition of chaos?*
—*We never give out information about the problems of Soviet agriculture.*

For other versions, see Jacobi, 1965:95; Kolasky, 1972:108; Benton and Loomes, 1976:144; and Hirche, 1977:140.

There are many jokes about this topic. For example, What are the four critical periods in Soviet agriculture? Spring, summer, autumn, and winter. See Hirche, 1964:250; Brandt, 1965:152; Durocher, 1965:71; Jacobi, 1965:73; Benton and Loomes, 1976:143; and Melor, 1979:37.

—*Is it true that the answers of Radio Erevan are printed all over the world?*
—*In principle, no. They are not printed in the Soviet Union.*

For another version, see Schiff, 1969:121.

—*Is it possible to introduce communism into Switzerland?*
—*In principle, yes, but it would be a pity.*

This is an extremely widespread and popular joke. The punch line varies somewhat. In another Romanian version, the ending is "But what for?" (Dor and Federmann, 1964:278). A Czech version ends with "But it would be a pity to ruin such a beautiful country," Beckmann, 1969:83, and Swoboda, 1969:13. For versions similar to the above text, see Hirche, 1964:294; Brandt, 1965:150; Drozdzynski, 1974:53; Paruit, 1978:17; Larsen, 1980:86; and Dolgopolova, 1982:81. In a related joke, Holland or some other country is featured. "Is it possible to introduce socialism in one country, say Holland?" "Of course, but what have you got against Holland?" or "It's possible, but what did Holland ever do to you?" See Shenker, 1978:9, and Draitser, 1978:13. In another variant, the site is Monaco with the answer: "Yes, but why wish such a *great* misfortune on such a *small* country,"

Kolasky, 1972:57, and Durocher, 1965:183. For Hungarian versions about Liechtenstein, see Drozdzynski, 1974:193, and Isnard, 1977:21.

—Is it possible to introduce communism into Switzerland?
—In principle, yes, but then it would be better to live in another country.

This is certainly related to the preceding joke, but it seems to have separate existence with an identity of its own. For other versions of this joke, see "Communism," *News from Behind the Iron Curtain,* 3, no. 4 (April, 1954): 56; Kukin, 1962:[28]; Dor and Federmann, 1964:209; Hirche, 1964:294; Brandt, 1965:177; Durocher, 1965:79; Benton and Loomes, 1976:86; Meyer, 1978:102–3; Melor, 1979:220; and Kalina, 1980:226.

—Is it possible to introduce communism into our Armenian Republic?
—In principle, yes, but we would rather have it tried in the Georgian Republic.

For other versions, see Schiff, 1969:61, and Kalbouss, 1977:448.

—What's the present situation of the United States's economy?
—The economy of the United States is on the brink of a precipice.
—And what about the economic situation of the Soviet Union?
—According to comrade Khrushchev, the Soviet Union is catching up and trying to overtake the United States.

For other texts, see Kukin, 1962:[122]; Dor and Federmann, 1964:249; Winick, 1964:24; Brandt, 1965:143, 211; Durocher, 1965:117; Jacobi, 1965:38; Beckmann, 1969:104; Kolasky, 1972:67; Brunvand, 1973:186; Drozdzynski, 1974:95; Benton and Loomes, 1976:99; Hirche, 1977:132, 197; Meyer, 1978:61, 63; Paruit, 1978:155; Melor, 1979:48; and Kalina, 1980:176.

—Can Soviet men be trusted [not to defect] when they are sent on official trips?
—In principle, yes. Especially the cosmonauts.

For other versions, see Schiff, 1969:86, and Larsen, 1980:87.

—What is a string quartet?
—The Moscow Symphony Orchestra after it returns from a trip to the
West.

There is also an additional question: Why do the K.G.B. learn only string instruments? In a Czech version, a quartet is a symphony orchestra after a staff check [for loyalty]. See Kalina, 1980:86.

7
Our Socialist Brothers

Back home after the invasion of Czechoslovakia, allegedly under-taken to suppress a "counterrevolution," a Soviet soldier runs into a friend.
—How was it, Ivan? Did you see any counterrevolutionaries?
—Of course I did.
—Did Piotr come back with you?
—No, I lost track of him.
—But he was in the same unit as you, wasn't he?
—Yes, but he *didn't see any counterrevolutionaries.*

For other versions, all Czech, see anon., 1969a:28; Swoboda, 1969:46–47; Drozdzynski, 1974:166; Benton and Loomes; 1976:113; and Kalina, 1980:221.

————————————

—Why did the Russians come into Czechoslovakia?
—Because they were called in.
—And how long are they going to stay?
—Until they find the person who called them in.

For other versions, see Kolasky, 1972:24; Benton and Loomes, 1976:113; and Meyer, 1978:100.

————————————

—Is it true that in 1968 our armed forces were called in by the Czechs to defeat the forces of fascist reaction?
—In principle, yes, but there is one correction to be made: the request was made in 1939, but for bureaucratic reasons it could not be met until 1968.

132

The reference, of course, is to Hitler's annexation of Czechoslovakia in 1939 on the eve of World War II and to Czechoslovakia's plea for help which was unanswered. For other versions of the joke, see Schiff, 1969:89; Kolasky, 1972:24; Drozdzynski, 1974:166; Speier, 1975:53; Benton and Loomes, 1976:144; anon., 1977:790; Hirche, 1977:165; Paruit, 1978:131; Melor, 1979:67; and Kalina, 1980:215.

—*Is it true that our leaders have stopped the Czech deviation just by threatening with one finger?*
—*In principle, yes, but with the finger on the trigger.*

For other versions, see Schiff, 1969:94, and Kolasky, 1972:24.

—*Is it true that the next edition of the Soviet Encyclopaedia will have a chapter on the Soviet occupation of Czechoslovakia?*
—*In principle, yes, but you will have to look it up under "fraternal support to socialist states."*

For another version, see Schiff, 1969:103.

—*What's the definition of normalization?*
—*Sticking a knife in your back and keeping it there until the wound heals around it.*

For another version, see anon., 1969a:28.

A Czech is standing at the edge of a cliff [or edge of a river], saying over and over:
—*Thirty-two, thirty-two, thirty-two . . .*
A Russian official approaches him.
—*What are you doing?*
—*Thirty-two, thirty-two, thirty-two . . .*
—*Why are you saying "thirty-two"?*
—*Thirty-two, thirty-two, thirty-two . . .*
—*If you don't stop saying "thirty-two," I'm going to arrest you.*
Just as he is about to seize the Czech, the Czech pushes the Russian off the cliff and says:
—*Thirty-three, thirty-three, thirty-three . . .*

For Czech versions, see Filip and Steiger, 1977:38; Paruit, 1978:133; and Kalina, 1980:72–73. For an American version in which a migrant from West Virginia in Chicago tricks a Chicagoan into falling down a manhole into the sewer, see Ray Ginger, *Ray Ginger's Jokebook about American History* (New York: New Viewpoints, 1974), 20.

A few days after the invasion of Czechoslovakia in 1968 a young girl picks up a Russian soldier and invites him to her home. She offers him drinks, then they go into the bedroom. After they have undressed, the girl excuses herself for a minute and goes to the bathroom. The Russian soldier waits for a while, then he becomes impatient and calls her. No answer. He goes to the bathroom and finds it empty. So is the whole house. Frustrated, he wants to leave, but he realizes that all his clothes, including his uniform are gone. In desperation, he wraps himself up in a bed sheet like in a burnous and jumps out of the window. Fortunately, a group of Arabs is just passing by, and he hopes to hide among them. As he comes closer, he hears someone in the group saying in Russian:
—Look, Ivan, here comes another one!

The friendship between the peoples of Czechoslovakia and Romania has historic roots. Both nations share the common fate of having tried for centuries to gain or maintain their independence against heavy odds. In 1968 Romania was the only country of the Warsaw Pact signatories which did not take part in the invasion of Czechoslovakia. This has led to a deepening of the friendly feelings between the two peoples due on the one hand to the sympathy the Romanians felt for their unfortunate neighbor and on the other to the gratitude of the Czechs for Romania's courageous stand.

Within one day after the invasion of Czechoslovakia, jokes connected with it were already circulating in Romania. Romania, with its own fears of the Soviet Union, could and can readily identify with the plight of Czechoslovakia. This may help explain the special pleasure Romanians have in telling jokes about Czechoslovakia.

Soon after the invasion, an international meeting is held in Moscow. During a break an American, a Frenchman, and a Russian have a friendly talk. The discussion turns to their holiday plans.
The American begins:
—I have bought four plane tickets to fly with my family over to Europe.

The Frenchman continues:
—My family plans to make a trip through all of Europe by car.
The Russian adds:
—We Russians travel abroad only by tank.

For other versions, see Kolasky, 1972:118; Paruit, 1978:127–28; and Kalina, 1980:220.

—What does it mean when you dream about tanks?
—You'll be visited by your brother.

In another version of this oneirocritical joke, the same question is answered "Friends" are coming. See Kolasky, 1972:22. Fears of a Soviet visit pervade eastern Europe generally. One joke purports to be an Intourist advertisement: "Visit the Soviet Union before the Soviet Union visits you." See Davies, 1981:155.

The Lord appeared one night before an old woman in Prague.
—I want to reward you for your pious and charitable life. I shall grant you three wishes.
—I wish, said the old woman, that the eight hundred million Chinese would come to Prague and then go back.
—And your second wish?
—I wish that the eight hundred million Chinese would come to Prague and then go back.
—The same? What about your third wish?
—I wish that the eight hundred million Chinese would come to Prague and then go back.
—Your wishes will be granted. But why do you want the Chinese to come three times to Prague?
—Just imagine what the Soviet Union will look like after the eight hundred million Chinese have passed through it six times!

For other versions also set in Czechoslovakia, see Kolasky, 1972:48; Drozdzynski, 1974:168–69; Benton and Loomes, 1976:115; Hirche, 1977:144–45; Meyer, 1978:98; Paruit, 1978:144; Kalina, 1980:204; and Larsen, 1980:101–2. For a version set in Hungary, see Dolgopolova, 1982:37.

An American, a Russian, and a Czech arrive at the same time at the gates of heaven. Before admitting them, St. Peter granted each one a last wish.

The Russian:

—I'd like to see New York blown to pieces by an H bomb.

The American:

—I'd like to see Moscow blown to pieces by an H bomb.

The Czech:

—I'd like a cup of coffee, please.

St. Peter was puzzled.

—Is that all? he asked, you can have all the coffee you want once you're in. Why not ask for something more special?

—No, thank you. A cup of coffee will be excellent while I wait for you to serve the other two gentlemen.

For other versions, see Dor and Federmann, 1964:252; Brandt, 1965:252; Beckmann, 1969:142; Swoboda, 1969:9; Kolasky, 1972:27; Drozdzynski, 1974:125; Benton and Loomes, 1976:153; Meyer, 1978:97; Paruit, 1978:130–31; Melor, 1979:66; and Dolgopolova, 1982:25–26. This joke is almost certainly an updated version of one current in Nazi times. In one text, Hitler, Stalin, and Churchill, not clear about each other's goals, ask God to serve as a neutral arbitrator. God asks Hitler, "So what do you intend to do?" I will destroy bolshevism." God asks Stalin, "And what do you intend to do?" "I will destroy national socialism." God asks Churchill, "And what is your wish?" "I will conclude with the wishes of the previous speakers." See Gamm, 1979[1963]:109, and Hirche, 1964:184–85. For another version (with Roosevelt, Stalin, and Churchill), see Durocher, 1965:169–70.

In Budapest in 1956 the Hungarian uprising has been crushed by Russian tanks, and the general condition of the city with its heaps of rubble and its battered buildings speaks for itself with respect to the friendly assistance given to Hungary by the Soviet Union.

Two men meet on the street.

—You know, come to think of it, we Hungarians are a very lucky people.

—What? You don't mean you've become one of them?

—Oh no, but just think. The Russians came here as friends. Imagine what they'd have done if they came here as enemies.

For a Hungarian version, see "Good Intentions," *East Europe*, 6, no. 5 (May, 1957): 16.

Ionescu calls on his friends the Popescu family.
—Congratulations on your fine baby.
—Thank you. But you know, we are in desperate need of a baby carriage. Since you work at the "We Fight for Peace" perambulator factory, I thought that maybe . . .
—Well, you see, I can't do it all at once, but I can smuggle out a spare part today, another one tomorrow, and after a while, you'll be able to assemble your do-it-yourself perambulator.
Two months later, Ionescu visits his friends again.
—Have you managed to put it together?
—Sure, but which ever way I assemble the damn thing, it always comes out as a machine gun.

As noted previously, because of the general shortage of both agricultural and industrial goods, people try to meet their needs by either stealing or having friends steal for them from the institutions in which they are employed. For other versions of the joke, see "Machine Age Magic," *News from Behind the Iron Curtain,* 3, no. 10 (October, 1954): 38; Kukin, 1962:[69]; and Dolgopolova, 1982:35–36. For a version set in pre-Nazi Germany, see Larsen, 1980:37.

—Will there be any more wars when all countries have achieved communism?
—In principle, no, except if the struggle for peace makes the use of weapons necessary.

The invasion of Hungary and Czechoslovakia by the Soviet Union and the invasions of Viet Nam by China and Cambodia by Viet Nam disprove the Marxist theory that wars are the result only of capitalist exploitation and imperialism. For another version of this joke, see Schiff, 1969:102.

There are other versions of the dangers of "peace." A text reported from 1962: "Will there be war or will there be peace?" "There will not be a war, but the struggle for peace will be so violent that not one stone will be left on another." See Kolasky, 1972:69. For other texts, see Langnas, 1963:17; Winick, 1964:48: Durocher, 1965:71; Roberts, 1966:1; Drozdzynski, 1974:121; Draitser, 1978:68; Kalina, 1980:230; and Dolgopolova, 1982:41.

One evening a Romanian border guard invited his Yugoslav counterpart to come over to his sentry post for a drink. Inside the hut the

Yugoslav noticed a poster representing Tito licking Uncle Sam's boot while stretching out his hand into which Uncle Sam is lavishly pouring gold from a bag. He begins to laugh.

—What's so funny? asks the Romanian.

—We have a quite similar poster in our hut, answers the Yugoslav, only Gheorghiu-Dej is licking Stalin's backside, and he doesn't get any gold in return.

To appreciate this joke, one must know that in 1948 Tito, breaking with communist tradition, made overtures to the West. As a result, he was declared a traitor by the Soviet Union, and all its satellites soon followed suit. An abusive campaign of vilification was launched in all countries of the Eastern bloc. Among the most widely used epithets were bloodhound, henchman, bloody butcher of the Yugoslav people, and mercenary agent of imperialism.

Relations between Romania and Yugoslavia became tense, but the traditional friendship between the two peoples continued on an individual level. Gheorghiu-Dej was at that time the first secretary of the Romanian Communist party. For another Romanian version of the joke, see Benton and Loomes, 1976:117–18. For another version, see Melor, 1979:70. For a version with Bulgaria instead of Romania, see Durocher, 1965:127.

After Stalin's death the vilification campaign against Tito stopped abruptly, and in 1955 a few months after Stalin's reign of terror had been exposed, Khrushchev went to Belgrade to meet Tito and patch things up.

On his return trip he stopped for a short visit in Bucharest. As the Romanian leader greeted him at the airport, the effusive Khrushchev kissed him on both cheeks. Gheorghiu-Dej instinctively drew back. Then realizing that his gesture might be taken as an offense, he apologized by saying that he had a rash.

—Oh, never mind! answered Khrushchev, Tito had hemorrhoids.

For another version (in which the Queen of England withdraws her hand from a Russian dignitary), see Kolasky, 1972:75.

Question for Radio Erevan.

—Is it true that Yugoslavia is no longer a socialist country?

—In principle, yes, because people live too well there.

For another version, see Schiff, 1969:90.

In 1949 a Jew comes to his rabbi.
—Rabbi, there is so much propaganda lately against Tito. I don't understand. Is he still a Communist? Or is he a capitalist? Is he no longer a Soviet satellite? What about his independence?
—Well, you know I'm not interested in politics. But I am reminded of two friends of mine, each of whom has a daughter. They haven't seen each other for a while, and when they meet again, they naturally talk about their daughters.
—How is Rachel?
—Oh, she is doing very well. She is the secretary of a high-ranking executive, and she is working very hard for him. He dictates everything to her, and she has to type and work for him all day long. Unfortunately, she sometimes has to stay with him overnight, and he dictates to her, and sometimes she even goes with him to the mountains over the weekend, and he dictates to her again. But at least she is making a lot of money. She has a fur coat, jewels, and she even bought a house where we live together with her. But what about your *daughter?*
—My daughter is a whore too, only nobody dictates to her.

Question for Radio Erevan.
—Isn't the Berlin Wall, which has been built to protect socialism, unnecessary?
—In principle, yes, for even without it, no one will flee from West Berlin to East Berlin.

For another version, see Schiff, 1969:97. There are many east European jokes about the Berlin Wall or about closed borders in general. Most assume that if the walls were removed or if the borders were opened, everyone would leave. For example, Ulbricht delivers a speech. Everyone applauds, but an especially attractive young lady continues to clap loudly after the others have stopped. Flattered, Ulbricht calls her to the podium and asks her if she really enjoyed his speech that much. She says that she did. Delighted, Ulbricht offers to fulfill any wish that she might have. She asks Ulbricht to tear down the wall the next day. Ulbricht begins to smile and says, "Aha, you little flirt. I understand. You just want to be alone with me." See Abrahams and Wukasch, 1967:8. For other versions, see Swoboda, 1969:15–16;

Drozdzynski, 1974:174; Hirche, 1977:194–95; Meyer, 1978:46; Melor, 1979:201; Kalina, 1980:238–39; and Larsen, 1980:104. In a variant, one man says, "Did you know that Ulbricht has opened the entire border with the West for one day?" A second man says, "Really? Why?" "Because he wants to celebrate his birthday alone with his wife.' See Streit, 1964:28, and Jacobi, 1965:99. The same theme occurs in a Bulgarian joke: "Petur, if they open the borders, will you remain here?" "No, Ivan, why should I stay all alone in Bulgaria?" See "Bootleg Wry Humor," *New York Times,* 6 January 1964, 11. The same import is contained in a Romanian joke in which one Communist leader suggests to another, "Why don't we just remove the restrictions and allow the people to travel anywhere they want to?" The reply, "What, and have only the two of us left in Romania?" See Brunvand, 1973:187. In another version of this joke, Kosygin begins by suggesting to Brezhnev that Jews be allowed to emigrate freely. But Brezhnev objects that the Lithuanians would want to go too. And then the Ukrainians, the Latvians, etc. "What if they did?" "But, Aleksei, what do you think? Who would remain here besides you and me?" "That wouldn't be an issue," answers Kosygin, "because I would also go." See Drozdzynski, 1974:88.

—Do the East Germans love the Russians?
—In principle, yes. For the Russians have "liberated" them.
—And do they hate the Americans?
—Sure, because they *haven't liberated them.*

For other versions, see Sanders, 1962:22; Sulzberger, 1962:32; Dor and Federmann, 1964:271; Brandt, 1965:13; Jacobi, 1965:38; Drozdzynski, 1974:193; and Larsen, 1980:92.

An East German was asked:
—Have you any Stalinists in your country?
He replied:
—I shall give you the same answer that a cannibal from Malaysia gave when he was asked, "Have you cannibals?" "No," he answered, "We ate the last cannibal yesterday."

This joke is somewhat reminiscent of a Russian text: A reception took place in the Kremlin in honor of the chief of an African tribe.

Brezhnev shared some of his problems with his guest. "Tell me," he asked the chief, "how did you solve the 'Jewish problem' in your country?" "Well," the chief shrugged his shoulders, "We really don't have any Jewish problem. There *was* one Jew living in our country, but we ate him up." See Draitser, 1978:51, but this text lacks the paradoxical punch of the Romanian joke.

Question for Radio Erevan.
—Why did Albania of all socialist countries celebrate so enthusiastically the launching of the first Russian satellite?
—Because it has ceased to be the smallest satellite.

For other versions, see Dor and Federmann, 1964:282; Brandt, 1965:160; Parth and Schiff, 1972:82; Drozdzynski, 1974:212; Benton and Loomes, 1976:129; and Melor, 1979:72.

—Why was the May Day parade cancelled in Albania?
—Because the tank ran out of gas.

This is reminiscent of a Nazi joke dating from 1940 in which the Czechs were asked if, now that they were at war, they would help with their tank forces? They answered, "Shall we dispatch one or two tanks—or all three?" See Hirche, 1964:140.

—Which is the most peaceful country in the world?
—Bulgaria.
—Why?
—Because it never interferes in any country's internal affairs. Not even its own.

This joke was invalidated after the 1968 invasion of Czechoslovakia by the Warsaw Pact armies in which Bulgaria took part. In most other versions of the joke, it is Czechoslovakia which is said to be the most neutral state in the world. See anon., 1969a:28; Kolasky, 1972:24; Drozdzynski, 1974:167; anon., 1977:790; Meyer, 1978:25; Melor, 1979:67; and Kalina, 1980:216. For a version in which it is Hungary, see Paruit, 1978:15.

News about China during the Cultural Revolution:
—The Chinese have put a satellite into orbit. They managed this by mobilizing the entire population in the effort. One hundred million Chinese held the sling while another hundred million pulled back the rubber band.

In an East German variant, 24,489 Chinese jump on one end of a seesaw. See Brandt, 1965:208. For other versions, see Parry, 1966:38; Bregman, 1967:21; Swoboda, 1969:46; and Hirche, 1977:147. This and other jokes about China reflect the fear the Russians, as well as the peoples of the Eastern bloc, have of China because of its huge population.

———————————

More news about China:
—Again by mobilizing the entire population, they have sent three men to the moon. They managed it by standing on each other's shoulders.

For other versions, see "Jokes from Hungary," *East Europe,* 13, no. 10 (October, 1964): 47; Bregman, 1967:21; and Paruit, 1978:145–46.
Another favorite joke shows the Chinese conquering Russia by the ploy of surrendering: The Soviet Union and China went to war, and on the first day one million Chinese surrendered. On the second day two million more surrendered. On the third day another five million surrendered. On the fourth day Mao Tse-tung called up Khrushchev and inquired, "Do you give up now?" See Sulzberger, 1964:26. For other versions, see Brandt, 1965:153; Parry, 1966:38; Bregman, 1967:21; Drozdzynski, 1974:103; Hirche, 1977:145; Isnard, 1977:30; Paruit, 1978:146; and Kalina, 1980:203.

———————————

There is a terrible plague of rats in the Kremlin. There are millions of them. Brezhnev issues an order that all comrades are urged to do whatever they can to solve the problem. The leading chemists develop a formula which does kill a million rats, but there are more than ten million left. The biologists and physicists also try, but without success. Nothing works. Finally there is just one little man who says he can find a solution. He makes a mechanical rat, winds it up, and places it on the ground. All the millions of rats follow it into the river where they drown. Brezhnev is delighted and rewards the man with many rubles. As the man is about to leave, Brezhnev calls him over and whispers:

—You did well, but tell me, could you make a small mechanical Chinese?

For other versions, see Parry, 1966:38; Bregman, 1967:22; Drozdzynski, 1974:104; Hirche, 1977:148; and Kalina, 1980:124.

Brezhnev and Ceausescu are sitting at a table across from each other. Each has his elbows on the table with his chin supported by his two hands. Brezhnev without moving his hands wags his right index finger at Ceausescu [as if to warn him about getting out of line with Soviet policy]. Ceausescu replies without moving his hands by pulling the corners of his eyes towards his ears so as to make them slanting [i.e., like the eyes of the Chinese].

—What does a cautious man do?
—He learns how to eat matzos with chopsticks.

For a Polish version, "we might as well learn to eat caviar with chopsticks," see Parry, 1966:41. For other versions of eating caviar with chopsticks, see Winick, 1964:62; and Isnard, 1977:19. In another Polish version, the optimist is learning American (English); the pessimist is learning to eat with chopsticks. See Paruit, 1978:146. In a Russian version, Brezhnev has a nightmare: a Czech was sitting in Red Square eating matzos—with chopsticks, Dolgopolova, 1982:16.

—What's the difference between an optimist and a pessimist?
—The optimist learns Russian, the pessimist learns Chinese.

This joke enjoyed wide circulation in Romania during the Cultural Revolution in China. For other versions, see Kukin, 1962:[125]; Dor and Federmann, 1964:290; Brandt, 1965:207; Durocher, 1965:131; Parry, 1966:15; Swoboda, 1969:35; Hirche, 1977:144; and Kalina, 1980:205.

In former days, optimists were those who learned English, pessimists were those who learned German, and realists learned Russian. In recent days, optimists still learn English, pessimists now learn Russian, while the realists learn Chinese.

For other versions, see Bregman, 1967:22; Schiff, 1969:100; and Schiff, 1975:61.

—How does a Russian cat scare her kittens when they don't want to go to sleep?
—By saying "Mao, Mao, Mao."

For a similar joke based upon the same pun: "It is being said in Moscow that the authorities ordered all cats to be exterminated because they could not stand listening to 'Mao, Mao, Mao,' all night long." See Jacobi, 1965:69; Bregman, 1967:22; and Schiff, 1969:33. Another Russian joke is a bit more pessimistic. Two cats are on a Moscow roof. "Miaou," says the first cat. "Maooo," says the second. "What's the matter with you?" asks the first cat. "Quiet," replies the second. "Don't breathe a word to anybody. I'm learning Chinese." See Parry, 1966:15. In a variant, two cats meet in a Moscow gutter. The optimist goes "Miaou"; the pessimist goes "Mi Ha-ou." See Paruit, 1978:146.

In December 1963.
—Did you hear there's been an important change in Chinese policy?
—No, what?
—Until recently they were against a Kennedy-Khrushchev meeting. Now they are all for it.

For a Polish version of this example of sick humor which followed the tragic assassination of President Kennedy, see Bregman, 1967:22; for another version, see Kolasky, 1972:11.

Ionescu enters a food store and asks for a package of tea.
—Russian tea or Chinese tea? asks the vendor.
—On second thought, I'd rather have some coffee, please.

For earlier Romanian versions, see Parry, 1966:41, and Drozdzynski, 1974:209. For Polish versions of this joke which so succinctly describes the delicate balancing act required of east Europeans with respect to Russia and China, see Durocher, 1965:132; Bregman, 1967:22; Isnard, 1977:21; and Paruit, 1978:145. For a Czech version, see Beckmann, 1969:142; for a Hungarian version, see Jacobi, 1965:18. For a version set in Yugoslavia, see Dor and Federmann, 1964:290; for an East German version, see Brandt, 1965:207. For other versions, see Hirche, 1964:274; Schiff, 1969:101; Benton and Loomes, 1976:134–35; Hirche, 1977:144; and Larsen, 1980:91.

8
Our Beloved Leaders

Question for Radio Erevan.
—Is it true that high-ranking communist officials live better than most capitalists?
—In principle, yes. This proves once again the basic inferiority of the capitalist system.

For another Romanian version, see Brunvand, 1973:186. For other versions, see Schiff, 1969:64, and Benton and Loomes, 1976:142.

—What's the definition of champagne?
—A popular drink in Romania consumed on behalf of the people by their appointed representatives.

For a Polish version, see Langnas, 1963:20–21. Brunvand reports the definition of a Spartak (a Czech compact automobile) as: "The people's vehicle, driven on behalf of the people by their appointed representatives." See Brunvand, 1973:186. In another version we find, "What is the Marxist-Leninist definition of a motorcar? A motorcar is a vehicle on four wheels driven by the toiling masses in the shape of their freely elected representatives." See Benton and Loomes, 1976:143, and Melor, 1979:152. For other versions, see Durocher, 1965:20; Schiff, 1969:52; Swoboda, 1969:14; Kolasky, 1972:65; and Kalina, 1980:195.

A poor old man is peddling some books on Red Square. Brezhnev sees him, stops, and moved by a sudden feeling of pity for the old man, asks:

—*How's business?*

—*Could be better. I can barely sell one or two books a day. But I'm thinking, maybe if you could give me some pictures of you to put on the covers, I'd have a better chance of selling them.*

Brezhnev wants to help, so he gathers all of his spare pictures and sends them to the peddler. Soon sales are soaring; all the books are sold in a day. Next day, no more pictures, no more sales. The man decides to take a chance. He goes to the Kremlin, asks to see Brezhnev, and begs for some more pictures. Brezhnev doesn't have any more left, but flattered by his popularity and being willing to help, he fishes out his family album and gives the old man many pictures of him with his family.

Again business flourishes, but again the peddler runs out of pictures. So again he goes to Brezhnev for help. This time, the first secretary, completely out of personal pictures, offers him photographs of the Central Committee of the Communist party.

This time, when the peddler tries to display his books, the K.G.B. appears on the scene and arrests him.

—*Look here, we knew you were protected by Brezhnev, so we didn't object when first you sold* The Idiot *by Dostoevski, nor when you sold Hugo's* Les Misérables. *But this time you've gone too far, trying to sell* Ali Baba and the Forty Thieves *with the Central Committee of the Communist party on the cover.*

In a Czech variant, the occupation troops in Czechoslovakia invite all inhabitants to an extraordinary ballet performance with pantomime entitled *Ali Baba and the 400,000 Thieves.* See Kalina, 1980:215.

—*Is it true that half of the members of the Central Committee are idiots?*

—*Wrong. Half of the members of the Central Committee are not idiots.*

For another version, see Schiff, 1969:74.

—*How can you expect anything to go right in a country governed by a Central Committee of which half the members are incapable of anything?*

—*Oh, but this is largely compensated for by the fact that the other half is capable of everything.*

For Russian versions, see Winick, 1964:50; Draitser, 1978:75.

Romulus Zaroni, minister of agriculture, speaks to Petru Groza, the prime minister:
—*Will you play a game of ting-tong with me?*
—*You fool, you mean Ping-Pong, not ting-tong.*
—*Come on, I won't be caught again. I already made a fool of myself about tennis.*

During the first few years of communism in Romania, one of the most popular subjects for jokes was the minister of agriculture, Romulus Zaroni, the only peasant who had risen to a high position in the government. Reportedly, he had a lot of common sense and, most unusual for a member of a communist government, he also had a good sense of humor, enjoying the jokes at his expense as well as anyone. However, his rural origin made him an easy target. In the above joke, the initial vowel in the Romanian pronunciation of "penis" is similar to the one in "tennis."

Zaroni must attend an opera gala for a group of foreign visitors. Prime Minister Petru Groza instructs him:
—*You must wear your formal suit, and don't forget to take a bath and change your underclothes, including your socks.*
At the gala Zaroni indeed makes a good appearance. However, after a while Groza becomes aware of an unpleasant odor in the box.
—*Zaroni, he asks, did you take a bath as I told you?*
—*Sure I did.*
—*Then you haven't changed your socks.*
—*There, I knew you wouldn't believe me. That's why in order to prove it, I took the old pair along in my pocket. Here they are.*

The theme of this joke is similar to one which also makes fun of unwashed peasants. A listener asks Radio Erevan "what should a pair of collectivist farmer newlyweds do on the first night of marriage not to dirty the bed?" Radio Erevan's answer: "Wash their feet." See Dundes, 1971:53. For another version, see Kalina, 1980:230.

Zaroni runs into an old friend whom he hasn't seen since communism took over in Romania.
—*Hi, Mitica, how are you doing? Where are you working?*

—I'm doing fine, but I'm not really working.

—How do you make a living then?

—By gambling. I make a good living from winning bets.

—Oh, come on. One cannot live from bets.

—Why not? I can prove it to you if you're willing to accept my bet.

—O.K. What's your bet?

—I bet you a hundred lei that in a week from now you'll have a boil on your ass.

—Agreed. But I warn you, you're going to lose. I have never had any boils.

—I'm ready to take the risk. See you next week.

For a few days, Zaroni forgets about his friend. But as the day in question approaches, he examines the area carefully and, to be on the safe side, swabs it with iodine. When Mitica calls on the appointed day, Zaroni is quite at ease. As he examines his friend, Mitica exclaims:

—Why did you use that colored stuff? I can't see very well.

They go to the window, and Mitica draws the curtain open. He examines his friend once more and then hands him a hundred lei bill.

—You win. Here's your money.

—But this still doesn't explain how you make a living.

—Oh, that's simple. I've bet a hundred lei with each of the sixty families from the surrounding apartment buildings that today they would be able to see the minister's naked ass at this window.

For a version set in Czechoslovakia, see Benton and Loomes, 1976:137–38. This is a standard joke popular in the West. For a representative text, see Andrew L. Cleveland, *Dirty Stories for All Occasions* (New York: Galahad Books, 1980), 20–21.

At a conference Zaroni notices how fresh and dapper some of the foreign delegates look, even when they have worked late into the night. He makes inquiry to discover how they manage it, and an aide tells him they use "eau de toilette."

—What's that? asks Zaroni.

—Toilet water, comrade Minister.

Next evening at a reception Zaroni appears with a bump on his head.

—What happened? asks Petru Groza.

—I tried the trick with the toilet water, and the lid fell on my head.

For a Czech version (told about Mrs. Novotný), see Beckmann, 1969:94.

The jokes about Zaroni were ascribed to a well-known Romanian writer. The minister summoned him one day to his office.
—Are you the author of the joke about ting-tong?
—Yes, I am.
—And the one about the socks?
—Yes, I'm the author.
—And the one about . . . and the one about . . .
—Yes, I made them up.
—But, sir, don't you know I am a minister?
—Sorry, this bad joke has been made by somebody else.

In a version set in Hungary, Brezhnev sends for Kohn who is known in Budapest for his jokes. Kohn arrives at the Kremlin at the prescribed hour, but Brezhnev isn't there. While Kohn waits, he admires the magnificently furnished rooms. Brezhnev finally arrives, apologizing for his lateness. Kohn explains that he has enjoyed seeing the beautiful paintings, carpets, etc. Brezhnev agrees that the house is beautiful and says the government is working so that all workers will have similar houses. Kohn, annoyed, says, "Tell me, comrade Brezhnev, did you bring me here to tell you jokes or so that I could listen to yours?" See anon. 1977:714 (= Paruit, 1978:174–75). For another Hungarian version, see Benton and Loomes, 1976:111. For other versions, see Winick, 1964:52; Brandt, 1965:227–28; Durocher, 1965:180–81; Jacobi, 1965:147; Kolasky, 1972:8; Shenker, 1978:9; and Kalina, 1980:177–78. In a modern Greek version, Papadopoulos questions a man known for telling lots of anti-junta jokes. The man admits he knows many funny stories about the government. Papadopoulos says, "And do you know that it is illegal to criticize the new government and that our glorious regime will last one hundred years?" "No," said the man, "that joke I hadn't heard." See Orso, 1979:13–14. A joke based on a similar theme maintains that dictators collected not only anecdotes about themselves but also those individuals who related them. See Kolasky, 1972:12. For other versions, see Hirche, 1964:295; Brandt, 1965:152–53; Swoboda, 1969:22; Drozdzynski, 1974:51, 185; Schiff, 1975:73–74; Benton and Loomes, 1976:104; Levy, 1976:23, 25; and Melor, 1979:136.

A Romanian Jew emigrates to Israel. At customs where his few personal belongings are thoroughly searched, the customs officer is amazed to see a framed portrait of Ana Pauker [at the time foreign minister and probably the most hated woman in the country].

—What did you take that for?
—As a reminder . . . just in case I ever get homesick.

For another Romanian version (with a picture of Ceausescu), see Paruit, 1978:52. For a Hungarian version (with a picture of Janos Kadar), see Luray, 1957:16. For a Polish version (with a picture of "Bierut, the Polish Stalin") see Langnas, 1963:20; for Czech versions (with a photograph of comrade Novotný), see Beckmann, 1969:64, and Swoboda, 1969:38; for a Czech version (with Husák), see Kalina, 1980:29. For older versions in which a German Jew takes a bust of Hitler, see Speier, 1975:54, and Benton and Loomes, 1976:65. For a Russian version (with a picture of Krushchev), see Durocher, 1965:149; for a Russian setting (with a picture of Brezhnev), see Melor, 1979:211; for a Russian version with the Soviet leaders not specified, see Dolgopolova, 1982:73.

Two friends talk over a drink in a restaurant.
—What do you think of Ceausescu?
—Not here, with so many people around.
—O.K., let's go outside.
In the street, the same question is asked.
—Are you crazy? In a crowded street where anyone could overhear us?
—Well, let's go to an empty park.
Finally, with nobody around, the man asks his friend again:
—Now tell me what you think of Ceausescu.
—Well, frankly, believe it or not, I like him.

For versions about Ulbricht, see Benton and Loomes, 1976:106; Melor, 1979:135–36; Kalina, 1980:239; and Larsen, 1980:95; for a version about Tito, see Meyer, 1978:43–44; for a version about Novotný, see Beckmann, 1980:87. In an East German variant an official, right before a party meeting, is asked where he stands on the Soviet Union. "Do you really want to know what I think?" he asks cautiously. "Of course." "Really?" the official says incredulously. "No subterfuge," admonishes the questioner. "Fine," says the official encouraged, "But you must absolutely keep this to yourself." "What do you mean?" says the questioner a little annoyed. "Will you definitely report this no further?" "Hell no!" Then the official, after warily checking that the surrounding comrades might not hear, whispers into the other man's ear, "Positive!" See Jacobi, 1965:114. This joke goes back to the Nazi era. In one version Hitler in 1942 wants to find out for himself what the people think of him. He gets a wig, trims his beard, and goes into the streets. He asks the first person he meets, "What do you think of the Führer?" The man whispers, "That I can't tell you here in the streets," and he leads Hitler into a sidestreet, takes him to a hotel, goes with him to a room, looks under the bed, locks the door, checks the wardrobe, and covers the telephone with a pillow. Then he approaches Hitler and whispers in his ear, "I am sympathetic to the Führer." See Gamm, 1979[1963]:89–90.

Ceausescu orders a sculptor to make a bust of him. When the statue is completed, all the party officials are there for the unveiling. But behold! It turns out that Ceausescu's bust has woman's breasts. Asked for an explanation, the sculptor says:
—One breast sustains (nourishes) the working class, the other the working peasantry.
—And what about the intellectuals?
—Well, comrade, the order was only for a bust!

"Se adapa" in Romanian means to drink (typically referring to cattle), but it can also mean "to take in spiritual sustenance from." As for the insulting gesture alluded to for intellectuals, it is a widespread one. See, for example, Heinz-Eugen Schramm, *LMIA* (Gerlingen, 1967).

Ceausescu has taken to his private residence some of the historic and artistic treasures of the nation including, among others, some centuries-old handwoven carpets which had been preserved in the Black Church in Brasov, one of the oldest gothic churches in the country, dating from the fourteenth century.
A Central Committee member calls on Ceausescu at his home. Upon seeing the famous carpets, he forgets himself to the point of exclaiming:
—Oh, my God!
—C'mon, old man, in private you may address me as comrade First Secretary.

Ceausescu's speeches, like those of all communist heads of state, are long and boring. A friend once advised him that making his speeches shorter would increase the chances of getting their message across. Ceausescu took the advice and asked his secretary to prepare a twenty-minute speech for his next public appearance. But as he read it, he went on and on for a whole hour. After the meeting, Ceausescu scolded his secretary for not having obeyed his orders.

—But, comrade First Secretary, came the answer, the speech I wrote was for only twenty minutes, but as is customary, I handed you three copies.

For a Polish version told about Gomulka, see Kolasky, 1972:38–39.

Three physicians are waiting at the gates of heaven. St. Peter checks out the new arrivals.

—Are any of you psychiatrists?

—I am, says one of them.

—Walk right in. You're welcome. You see, it's rather awkward, but we've had some trouble lately with . . . well, with the boss. He thinks he's Ceausescu.

This is a standard joke widespread in the United States where it was told in the 1950s, for example, about General MacArthur. For a version about France's de Gaulle, see Hirche, 1977:103. For a Russian version in which God thinks he's Stalin, see Winick, 1964:19. For a later version set in a Russian psychiatric clinic in which a megalomaniac under treatment used to think he was God but now thinks he is Brezhnev, see Isnard, 1977:53.

During an official visit to Paris, Mrs. Ceausescu is shown around the Louvre. She stops in front of a painting.

—Is this a Matisse?

—No, madam, it is a Renoir.

After a while she stops again.

—Is this a David?

—No, madam, this is a Corot.

Another stop.

—Is this a Picasso?

—No, madam, it is a mirror.

For a Czech version told about Brezhnev in Prague, see Filip and Steiger, 1977:42.

Khrushchev wanted to spend an evening as an ordinary citizen, so he disguised himself and went to a movie theater. As always, the program began with a newsreel.

As soon as a picture of Khrushchev appeared on the screen, the audience stood up, cheering and applauding. Khrushchev sat in his seat, moved and flattered by this outburst of affection.

His neighbor whispered in his ear:

—You crazy or something? Why don't you do like everybody else? No one gives a damn for the fool on the screen, but why look for trouble?

For other versions, see Winick, 1964:14; Swoboda, 1969:43; Drozdzynski, 1974:162; Benton and Loomes, 1976:94; Isnard, 1977:61; and Paruit, 1978:52.

During a state visit to the Soviet Union, Eisenhower tells Khrushchev his surprise at seeing so many drunks on the streets of Moscow. But the Soviet boss, never ready to accept criticism from a capitalist, vows to prove to Eisenhower that there are just as many drunks on the streets of Washington. Eisenhower is so certain that Khrushchev is wrong that on the Soviet boss's first visit to Washington, he hands him a pistol and invites him to shoot any drunk he might meet on the street.

Next morning, the Washington Post *carries the headline:*
 SMALL FAT GANGSTER SHOOTS
 SOVIET AMBASSADOR TO THE U.S.

For other versions, see Kolasky, 1972:79, and Paruit, 1978:124.

Khrushchev is being driven in a limousine in a rural area of Czechoslovakia. Suddenly, the car strikes and kills a pig which has wandered onto the road. The chauffeur asks Khrushchev if he wants to drive on, and Khrushchev replies:

—No, we'd better go up to the nearest farmhouse and pay some damages.

And so Khrushchev sends his chauffeur off to the farmhouse on the hill with instructions to offer the farmer some compensation. A half hour passes, and the chauffeur does not return. Then another half hour. Khrushchev begins to wonder what has happened. Still another half hour passes, and finally Khrushchev sees the chauffeur returning. To his surprise, the chauffeur is staggering under the weight of all sorts of packages and gifts.

—What happened? asks Khrushchev, I sent you to pay them.
—I don't know, replies the chauffeur, all I said to them was: I have Khrushchev in the car and I killed the pig.

For a 1943 German text told about Hitler in which the chauffeur runs over a dog rather than a pig, see Hirche, 1964:147. Hirche observes (1977:29) that this is one of a number of anti-Nazi jokes which has been transformed into a popular anti-communist jibe. For another version about Hitler (and a pig), see Benton and Loomes, 1976:66. For an East German version involving Ulbricht and a dog, see Abrahams and Wukasch, 1967:8. For a modern Greek version told about Papadopoulos, see Orso, 1979:6; for versions about Brezhnev, see Paruit, 1978:55, and Kalina, 1980:106.

A Romanian scientist on official business in Moscow is invited by a Russian colleague to his home. While continuing the scientific discussion begun at the research institute, the Russian generously serves vodka to his Romanian colleague.
—Under socialism, he says, we Russians are never short of vodka.
—Thank God! says the Romanian.
—We Russian scientists never say "thank God." We say "thank Stalin."
—But what if Stalin dies?
—Then we'll say thank God!

For similar Russian versions, see Wolfe, 1951:13; Dor and Federmann, 1964:221; Hirche, 1964:268; Winick, 1964:48; Brandt, 1965:21; Durocher, 1965:109; Drozdzynski, 1974:47; Benton and Loomes, 1976:86–87; Draitser, 1978:21; Melor, 1979:168; and Beckmann, 1980:22. For a version with Khrushchev instead of Stalin, see Kukin, 1962:[22]. For versions with Brezhnev, see Isnard, 1977:63, and Paruit, 1978:47. For a version with Tito, see Meyer, 1978:48. In an earlier version from Nazi Germany, two individuals approach a crucifix. One says to the other, "Heil Hitler." The second individual chides the first, "In such a case, one ought to say 'Praised be Jesus Christ.'" "That I will only say when the former hangs there." See Gamm, 1979[1963]:112–13. For a version told in England about Hitler, see also Gamm, 91.

At school the teacher explains the meaning of the word "tragedy." To see if the children understand, the teacher asks them to give some examples.

A child says:
—If a ship carrying a valuable cargo sinks, that's a tragedy.
—No, says the teacher, that's not a tragedy, it's only a loss.
Another child says:
—When two cars collide and people are killed in both cars, it's a tragedy.
—No, this is a misfortune, says the teacher. It's still not a tragedy.
Now Bula raises his hand.
—Stalin's death was a tragedy, he says.
—That's a good example, says the teacher. Can you explain why it was a tragedy?
—Because Stalin's death was neither a loss nor a misfortune.

This joke circulated soon after Stalin's death, long before his myth had been debunked. For earlier versions, see "The Tragic Sense," *News from Behind the Iron Curtain*, 3, no. 7 (July, 1954): 20, and Hirche, 1964:229–30. In another text, a teacher asks his students, "What is a stroke of destiny?" "If I lost my stamp collection," explained Ivan. "No, that would be a loss," replied the teacher. "If I broke a windowpane playing ball," yelled Jan. "No that would simply be a pity." "If Gomulka died," cried Hetel. "Right," responded the teacher "that would neither be a pity nor a loss." See Melor, 1979:169. This joke appears to have Nazi antecedents. In one German text dating from 1939, a rabbi is asked whether he knows the difference between a catastrophe and a misfortune. "That is easy to answer," said the rabbi. "If the ceiling in the parliament chamber collapses and buries the entire Reich's government, that is a catastrophe, but it is no misfortune!" See Hirche, 1964:135.

In Hungary the following dialogue is heard.
—What's the difference between an accident and a tragedy?
—Look. If the Saint Margareth Bridge collapses and there are no people on it, it's an accident, but no tragedy. If there are people on it, it's a tragedy.
—And what if the A.V.O. building [the secret police building facing the bridge] collapses?
—That would not be an accident and, sure as hell, not a tragedy.

This is obviously a variant of the preceding text. For a Russian version, see Draitser, 1978:17. For another version, in which if a Russian falls into the water and there is not much one can do for him, it is an accident, but if he knows how to swim, it is a catastrophe, see Paruit, 1978:140. See also Dolgopolova, 1982:11.

After Stalin had been debunked, the central committee decided to remove his body from the mausoleum where it lay beside Lenin's. But they were undecided about what to do with it. Someone suggested sending it to Israel and fogetting about it, but Khrushchev opposed the suggestion:
—Don't you know they already had one resurrection there?

In a version reported in 1962, Khrushchev objects to Mikoyan's proposal to send Stalin's body to Israel: "Better not. I seem to recall that Israel is the place where, a long time ago, someone rose from the dead." See Sulzberger, 1962:32. For other versions, see Winick, 1964:16; Brandt, 1965:179; Beckmann, 1969:36; Kolasky, 1972:7; Drozdzynski, 1974:76–77; Isnard, 1977:52–53; Meyer, 1978:36; Paruit, 1978:59; Larsen, 1980:83; Kalina, 1980:236.

Question for Radio Erevan.
—What would have happened if Khrushchev had been assassinated instead of President Kennedy?
—We cannot say for sure, but one thing is certain: Onassis would never have married Mrs. Khrushchev.

For another Romanian text, see Brunvand, 1973:188. For other versions, see Drozdzynski, 1974:68; Schiff, 1975:71; Paruit, 1978:62; and Kalina, 1980:228.

Khrushchev and Ulbricht were once walking in Moscow. Khrushchev saw a little boy and asked him:
—Who is your father?
—Khrushchev.
—Who is your mother?
—The Soviet Union.
—And what would you like to be?
—A cosmonaut.
Some time later Khrushchev was on a visit to East Berlin. He and Ulbricht were again walking, and again they saw a little boy.
—Who is your father?

—Ulbricht.
—Who is your mother?
—The German Democratic Republic.
—And what would you like to be?
—An orphan.

In a Nazi text of 1944, a schoolboy is questioned by a local official: "Who is your father?" "Adolf Hitler." "Who is your mother?" "Germany." "And what do you want to be?" "An orphan." See Hirche, 1964:163. For an Austrian version which refers only to Hitler, see Dor and Federmann, 1964:184. For other versions about Ulbricht, see Streit, 1964:28; Brandt, 1965:234; Benton and Loomes, 1976:105; and Hirche, 1977:185. The joke can obviously be told about any dictator. For versions about Stalin, see Winick, 1964:22; Drozdzynski, 1974:44–45; and Melor, 1979:168; for a version about Brezhnev, see Isnard, 1977:34–35. For Polish versions about Gomulka, see Durocher, 1965:120, and Lo Bello, 1966:23–24. For a version about Tito, see Meyer, 1978:43; for a version about Spain's Franco, see García, 1977:9. For another version told about the Communist party as "father," see Paruit, 1978:188; for the Soviet Union as "father," see Dolgopolova, 1982:21.

—Do you know why our president has also taken over the presidency of the State Council?
—Why?
—Because he has finally realized that in Romania one cannot make ends meet on a single salary.

"All animals are equal, but some animals are more equal than others," wrote Orwell in his celebrated parody of communist states: *Animal Farm*. The leaders in communist countries as well as high ranking officials enjoy a comfortable life, one which their western counterparts could envy. In order to appreciate the irony of the above joke, one needs to keep this in mind plus the fact that the top leaders are above the law—in this case the one forbidding double employment. For Czech versions of the joke, see Beckmann, 1969:110, and Swoboda, 1969:21. For a version from Yugoslavia, see Lo Bello, 1966:26.

At the 150th anniversary of the birth of A. S. Pushkin, the Supreme Soviet has decided to build a new monument to the great Russian poet. A competition was announced for the best statue. After hundreds of proposals were examined, the winner was selected.

His statue showed Stalin reading a luxury edition of Pushkin's poems.

An early version of this joke is in pseudo riddle form: "On the stage is a full-length portrait of Stalin. In front of it, a lecturer talks about Stalin. A choir sings in praise of Stalin and poets recite works extolling him. What is it? Answer: A Pushkin memorial evening." See Dallin, 1949:15. In an interesting variant, the results of the USSR competition for the erection of a new statue of Pushkin are announced in the newspaper: second prize is Stalin reading Pushkin; first prize is Pushkin reading Stalin. See Paruit, 1978:171–72. For other versions of this popular joke, see Kukin, 1962:[14]; Dor and Federmann, 1964:216; Hirche, 1964:281; Winick, 1964:14; Brandt, 1965:129; Beckmann, 1969:21; Kolasky, 1972:3; Drozdzynski, 1974:47; Meyer, 1978:34; and Kalina, 1980:182.

—Why is there no pork on the market?
—Because all the swine hold high party positions.

For a Hungarian version in which the question, "Why is there no meat in the Soviet Union?" is answered "because the sheep work and the cows govern," see Isnard, 1977:18. In an East German variant, the answer to a similar question is "because the oxen sit in the government, the sheepsheads [=blockheads] work, and the swine sleep with the Russians." See Hirche, 1964:254; and Brandt, 1965:62. For a Czech version, see Beckmann, 1969:109. For other versions, see Durocher, 1965:46; and Kolasky, 1972:56.

9
Always the Jews

A son is born to a Jewish family in Romania. The family gathers to admire him, and each member feels compelled to make a prediction about the boy's future.
—With such looks he will surely be an actor.
—Oh, come on, look at his forehead. His prospects are to become a scientist.
—Did you hear how loud he screams? His prospects are to become an opera tenor.
Then along came an old bearded man who cut away all his prospects.

Like the knife used by the *mohel*, the traditional circumciser in Jewish tradition, this joke is double-edged. It refers to the lack of prospects for Jews in Romania. Since circumcision normally is performed soon after birth, the implication is being born a Jew means being born without prospects.

An applicant for a job is interviewed by the secret police official responsible for screening personnel.
—Name?
—Isaac Rabinovitch.
—Was your father a businessman?
—No.
—Have you or your parents ever owned land or a house?
—No.
—Good. Have you any relatives abroad?
—No.

—Have you ever been a member of the Iron Guard [the Romanian Fascist movement]?
—No.
—Nationality?
—Well, comrade, when it's yes, it has to be yes.

In all communist countries every person has to declare himself as belonging to a particular ethnic group, irrespective of whether it's the dominant group or a minority. This information is then entered on each individual's identity card and on his or her personal file under "nationality." Hence the word does not carry the meaning of citizenship as it does in the United States. A Jew belongs to the Jewish "nationality" even though he is a Romanian citizen. An ethnic Romanian has Romanian nationality. Because of the existence of discrimination, Jewish nationality (and for that matter Hungarian nationality too) is a definite liability in job applications. For another version of this joke, see Drozdzynski, 1974:40.

When the chief rabbi of Moscow died, Stalin asked that a list of candidates for the opening be submitted to him for approval. He began to read it: Aronovitch, Bernstein, Iacobocitch, Levy. . . . Stalin exclaimed:
—Who's the idiot who screened these guys? Can't you see they're a bunch of damn Jews?

In a variant, a slightly different selection process is described. "Is it because of anti-Semitic politics that the synagogue of Kychinev in Moldavia is closed?" "No, not at all, it is solely because there is no rabbi." "How can that be? Did no one present himself for the post?" "Oh . . . yes." "Then, how is that possible?" "The first candidate had his rabbinical diploma, but he was not a member of the Party. The second was indeed a member of the Party, but he did not have his diploma. As for the third, he had his diploma and his card, but, alas, . . . he was a Jew." See Melor, 1979:175–76. For other versions, see Brandt, 1965:176–77; Durocher, 1965:140–41; Jacobi, 1965:47; Beckmann, 1969:56; Kolasky, 1972:50; Drozdzynski, 1974:63; Benton and Loomes, 1976:89; Meyer, 1978:94; and Kalina, 1980:53.

Romanians hate the Russians so much that they automatically take sides with anyone opposed by the Russians.

The following discussion takes place between two Romanian friends during the 1967 Arab-Israeli war.
—*Did you hear the latest news about the great performance of the Israeli troops?*
—*I couldn't care less.*
—*How come? Yesterday you seemed to care a lot.*
—*Yes, but I just found out that all the Israelis are Jews.*

Two friends met in the street.
—*Hi, how are you, Moritz?*
—*Fine, I am helping to strengthen communism here in Romania.*
—*And how is your brother Isaac?*
—*He is in Moscow now. He is helping to strengthen communism in the Soviet Union.*
—*And your brother Sami?*
—*Oh, he's fine. He emigrated to Israel.*
—*Is he helping to strengthen communism there too?*
—*Meshugge? [Are you crazy] In his own country?*

For other versions, see Hirche, 1964:300; Durocher, 1965:147; Drozdzynski, 1974:107; Melor, 1979:221; Kalina, 1980:235–36; and Dolgopolova, 1982:23.

At four in the morning a line is forming in front of a meat market in Moscow. At eight a vendor appears, sees the length of the line, and says:
—*Comrades, we are sorry, there won't be meat enough for all these people. We have to ask all the Jewish comrades to leave.*
One hour later the vendor opens a window and says:
—*We are sorry, but we've been informed that we will receive less meat than expected. We must kindly ask all nonparty members to leave.*
When only party members are left in the line, the manager appears and says:
—*Comrades, now that we are among ourselves, I can tell you that owing to unpredicted circumstances, our allocation of meat has been cancelled. We won't have any meat this week.*
This time, the people get angry.
—*Damn those dirty kikes, they've been favored as usual by being warned first.*

For other versions, see Meyer, 1978:69–70; Paruit, 1978:149–50; Melor, 1979:197, 151–52; Beckmann, 1980:51; Kalina, 1980:54–55; and Dolgopolova, 1982:69–70.

———————————

An inspector rings at the door of an apartment in a posh apartment building.
—How many rooms do you occupy?
—Four rooms.
—How many persons?
—Two.
—You will have to give up three of your rooms to the agency to be assigned to a family of working people.
—How dare you? Don't you know I'm the town responsible? [In Romanian communist officialese, "responsible" means "official in charge of."]
—Oh, I'm awfully sorry, comrade responsible, please accept my apologies.
The inspector goes to the other floors, and at each apartment a similar dialogue takes place. Frustrated because he cannot requisition any room (which would almost certainly result in receiving huge bribes from those to whom the rooms were newly assigned) but more cautious, the inspector calls at the last apartment.
—How many rooms do you occupy?
—Five.
—How many persons?
—Three.
—Name and occupation, please.
—Goldenberg, responsible for the republic.
The inspector leaves the premises with a thousand apologies. Goldenberg's wife turns to him:
—What did you mean by "responsible for the republic"?
—Well, when all this mess they call a republic finally breaks down, who do you think will be held responsible for the mess? Goldenberg.

This joke refers to the early years of communist rule in Romania when inspectors from the Living Space Agency were checking all apartments to see if anyone lived in "excessive" space, that is, in excess of the legally allowed ten square yards per person. If excessive space was found the inspectors made a note of it, and in no time they brought in another family to occupy it. Of course, individuals with high-ranking positions were not obliged to share their apartments.

For a Czech version of the joke, see Beckmann, 1969:59–60. The inevitable scapegoating of Jews is a favorite topic in jokes, especially among Jews. Attempts of Jews to disguise their identity in order to avoid scapegoating, although attesting to the great adaptive powers of Jews, invariably failed. The following text is representative: During the purge of high party officials, Gomulka sends for Goldberg. "Sorry, comrade Goldberg, but I must relieve you of your post. I've just been told you have no high school diploma." "Ah, comrade Gomulka, just give me a couple of days!" Two days later Goldberg returns with a high school diploma. "Sorry, comrade Goldberg, but this position demands a college education." "Comrade Gomulka, give me another two days!" Two days later Goldberg returns with a college degree. "Sorry again, comrade Goldberg, even though you have a high school diploma and a college degree, there is a quota on Jews in this office." "Comrade, give me another couple of days!" Two days later Goldberg returns with a Catholic baptismal certificate. "Comrade Goldberg, I really must relieve you of your post. It is important that the world know that we do not discriminate—we also fire non-Jews." See anon., 1969b, 26–27. For another version, see Melor, 1979:180–81.

A man knocks at the door of a shabby house on the outskirts of Bucharest. An old man sticks his head out of the window.
—Does the tailor Rabinowitch live here?
—No.
—Who are you?
—Rabinowitch.
—And aren't you a tailor?
—Yes, I am.
—Then why did you say you didn't live here?
—You call this living?

The consistency of both name and occupation in this joke is noteworthy. For a version about tailor "Rabinowicz," see Kukin, 1962:[31]; for a version about a tailor named "Rabinowitsch," see Dor and Federmann, 1964:214. For a version about a tailor "Rabinovich," see Benton and Loomes, 1976:91. In one version, the tailor is named Salomon Grünberg. See Drozdzynski, 1974:52. In a variant without either the occupation or the name, an old Russian villager is asked his age by a communist census taker. His reply, "I'm twenty-seven" is clearly false, and he is further questioned by the official. The old man then says, "Well, I'm really seventy-two but these last forty-five years since the revolution—do you call this living?" See Winick, 1964:53.

Two Jews are traveling together in a train compartment. One of them is constantly wailing:
—Oi! Oi! Oi!
The other Jew finally explodes:
—Will you ever stop talking politics?

In a variant, the second Jew responds, "You're telling *me?*" For a Polish version, see anon., 1969b:26. For a version told about non-Jews (where the workers merely sigh or mutter syllabic exclamations), see Durocher, 1965:178, and anon., 1977:714. In an East German variant, one of two old men sitting on a park bench keeps spitting. Finally the other says, "Please, no political conversation, or I shall call the police." See Adolph Schalk, *The Germans* (Englewood Cliffs, N.J.: Prentice-Hall, 1971), 65. For a Hungarian parallel to this last text, see Jacobi, 1965:7. For other versions, see Winick, 19642:29; Durocher, 1965:157.

Stalin wanted to test the loyalty of his guard regiment. He picked one of its soldiers and asked:
—Ivan, would you shoot me?
—Me, comrade Stalin? I'd rather cut off my arms!
He picked another one.
—Piotr, would you kill me?
—Me, comrade Stalin? I'd rather shoot my own father!
Then he picked the Jewish drummer of the regiment:
—Goldenberg, would you shoot me?
—Me, comrade Stalin? Vat vit? Vit de drum??

Evidently this is an updated version of an older joke. For a version involving a Jew and the czar, see Dor and Federmann, 1964:202. For a version told about a Jew and Khrushchev, see Jacobi, 1965:65.

A Jew who has been fired and who has remained unemployed since is hungry and dejected. He meets a friend who has suffered a similar fate and yet who appears to be doing very well.

—Say, weren't you fired too?
—Sure I was.
—And how do you manage?
*—Well, you know that Pole who hid me during the German occupa-
tion . . . Now I can blackmail him with it.*

This joke probably originated in the period following the Polish government's actions in 1968. At that time the government unleashed a
very brutal anti-Semitic campaign, firing a large number of Jewish
specialists and officials, even threatening with dismissal Polish em-
ployees occupying important positions if they did not divorce their
Jewish wives. The period was also marked with acts of vandalism such
as the desecration of Jewish graves, attacks against synagogues, etc.
For Polish versions of the joke, see Drozdzynski, 1974:141, and
Meyer, 1978:96.

---

*Moshe, now an American citizen, takes a trip to Romania and visits
his old buddy Isaac whom he hasn't seen for twenty years.*
*—Isaac, old boy, why didn't you follow my advice and leave the
country as I did while the going was good?*
—Because of the three months.
—What do you mean?
*—It's like this. When I first saw the political trend in the country, I
told myself:—It's too absurd, most people are anti-Communists; this
cannot last more than three months, so why leave my country? Then
after the monarchy had been abolished, I told myself:—There are only
three months till the elections, and all this absurdity will come to an
end. After the elections had been rigged, I told myself:—People can't
take this. They'll do something; it can't take more than three months,
and all this shebang will crumble. Then when I realized that people no
longer had any power to do anything, I told myself that the West will do
something. We'll have some form of intervention before three months
pass, I said. And so on, and so on. Here I am with my life wasted
because I told myself again and again that such an absurdity cannot
possibly last more than three months.*
*—Listen Isaac, it's not too late; I can pull strings and get you out
right now, to come with me to America.*
—Meshugge? Now when there are only three months left?

A Polish joke based on the same theme is phrased in question form:
"How does a clever Jew speak to a dumb Jew? By telephone from Paris

to Warsaw." See Drozdzynski, 1974:141, and Melor, 1979:201. For a Czech version, see Swoboda, 1969:13.

A Jew applies for emigration to Israel. His boss who is notified at once by the passport bureau summons him to his office.
—You, comrade Goldenberg, a party member of the old guard, why on earth do you want to leave your country?
—For two reasons. First, the system won't last.
—Oh, c'mon, you know as well as I do that communist rule will last forever.
—That's the second reason.

For an earlier version of this joke, see "Two for the Road," *News from Behind the Iron Curtain*, 2, no. 2 (February, 1953): 63. For Polish versions, see Langnas, 1963:20; Levy, 1976:22; Hirche, 1977:156; and Meyer, 1978:91; for Hungarian versions, see Dor and Federmann, 1964:269–70; Benton and Loomes, 1976:110–11, and Melor, 1979:220. For a Czech version, see Drozdzynski, 1974:164–65; for Russian versions, see Winick, 1964:43; Draitser, 1978:67; and Dolgopolova, 1982:25.

A Jew comes to the rabbi.
—Tell me, rabbi, will they ever let us go?
—Well, my son, there are only two possible ways for it to happen: the natural way or by a miracle.
—What's the natural way?
—The sky will open, and an angel with a fiery sword will say: Let my people go!
—But rabbi, that would be a miracle.
—Oh no, any other way would be a miracle.

In a version of this joke set in Poland, Gierek visits the Pope in Rome and asks how to get rid of Soviet troops in his country. The Pope explains there are two ways: the natural and the supernatural. Gierek says he is a Marxist, and therefore he prefers the natural way. In that case, the Pope says, he can intercede with God so that the archangel Michael will chase the Russians out. Gierek, surprised at the natural means, asks what the supernatural means are. The Pope answers, "That the Russians leave of their own accord." See Paruit, 1978:139–

40. For versions set in Czechoslovakia, see Kolasky, 1972:27, and Kalina, 1980:218. For another version, see Durocher, 1965:148–49.

—*Did you know that the sale of slippers was prohibited?*
—*No, why?*
—*Because the Jews have announced they'll leave even if only in slippers.*

In 1951 a wave of emigration to Israel was announced. People allowed to leave could take along only a minimum of personal belongings, but this, of course, didn't deter the Jews from applying for emigration. In order to stem the rush to the passport bureau, Jews were called to special meetings at various institutions. At these meetings lengthy lectures were given on the advantages of living in a country which is developing socialism and the horrors of living in a capitalist country like Israel. The speakers even described the precarious conditions in the reception camps set up for immigrants in Israel which at that time consisted largely of tents which made life quite uncomfortable especially in the rainy season.

—*Moshe listens carefully and suddenly begins shaking his head as if in a dilemma.*

—*What is it, comrade Rabinowitch, you still have doubts as to where it's better for you to live?*

—*No, I was wondering—should I take my coat?—should I leave it behind?*

In the year 1990 a Soviet spaceship returns from a routine trip to the moon. After touching ground, the two astronauts Ivan and Moritz go right home.

Moritz is received by his wife.

—*Did you hear the latest? she asks. Rumor has it they will let us leave.*

10
The Future of an Illusion

Question for Radio Erevan.
—Is it true that communism appears now clearly at the horizon?
—In principle, yes. According to definition, the horizon is an imaginary line which recedes in the distance as we try to approach it.

For other versions of this joke, see Hirche, 1964:294; Winick, 1964:18; Brandt, 1965:144; Durocher, 1965:81; Beckmann, 1969:90; Schiff, 1969:62; Kolasky, 1972:121; Drozdzynski, 1974:80; anon, 1977:671; Paruit, 1978:7; Melor, 1979:217–18; and Kalina, 1980:77, 229.

Three cars are driving along in a line. In the first is Brezhnev; the second, Nixon; and the third, Ceausescu. The cars come to a fork in the road. Of course, Brezhnev turns to the left. Nixon turns to the right. Ceausescu signals to the left, but turns to the right.

For Romanian and Egyptian versions, see Paruit, 1978:11. For another version set in Romania, see Kalina, 1980:134. For a version from Yugoslavia, see Jacobi, 1965:145.

God was walking and he met Brezhnev who is weeping.
—Why are you weeping?
—Because Americans have a better standard of living.
—Don't feel bad, you are ahead in the space race. [This joke was collected in 1969 before the American lunar landing.] And you should be happy.

And God left him feeling much better. Then God walked further, and he met Nixon weeping.
—Why are you weeping?
—Because the Russians are ahead in the space race.
—But you have a better standard of living, so you should be happy.
Nixon felt consoled. Then God walked a little further and saw Ceausescu sitting on a step weeping. [long pause] And God walked over, sat down beside him, and began to weep too!

In a variant set in Yugoslavia, Ford, Brezhnev, and Tito, in a time of crisis, are each permitted to ask God one question. Ford asks when will the United States come out of the crisis? God replies, "In fifty years." Ford breaks into tears saying, "Oh, I will never see the day." Brezhnev asks when will the economic power of the USSR equal that of the United States. God replies, "In one hundred years." Brezhnev breaks into tears exclaiming, "Oh, I will never see the day." Tito asks when will the dinar be a strong currency. At these words, God breaks into tears saying, "Oh, I will never see the day." See Meyer, 1978:63, cf. Kalina, 1980:254 (Nixon, Pompidou, and Brezhnev). For another version set in Yugoslavia, see Hirche, 1977:176. In another version, Christ is sent back to earth by God to see what has happened in the two thousand years since his sacrifice. Christ goes first to Washington where he sees Carter with his head between his hands, crying, crying, crying. Christ asks him to explain and Christ consoles him. Then Christ goes to Moscow where he sees Brezhnev crying. He asks him to explain, and Brezhnev begins to explain the situation in Russia. Jesus listens attentively and then begins crying, crying, crying . . . See Paruit, 1978:183, and Kalina, 1980:42. For a Russian version told about Kennedy, de Gaulle, and Khrushchev, see Dolgopolova, 1982:11–12. For a Polish version (Johnson, Kosygin, Brezhnev, and Gomulka), see Jacobi, 1965:27.

It is the year 2000. In Washington, the capital of the Soviet Union, one Chinese says to another:
—Say, Li, when is your son's Bar Mitzvah?

Marx's ghost appears at the Moscow radio station.
—Comrades, could you put me on the air for a few seconds?
—Oh, comrade Marx, whenever you wish, for any length of time.

—Just a few seconds will do, thank you.
And Marx's voice is heard all over the world:
—Workingmen of all countries, forgive me!

For other versions, see Isnard, 1977:62–63 (about Lenin); Meyer, 1978:34–35; Kalina, 1980:76; and Dolgopolova, 1982:105.

Bibliography

Abrahams, Roger D., and Charles Wukasch
1967 Political Jokes of East Germany. *Tennessee Folklore Society Bulletin* 33:7–10.

Anon.
1969a Gallows Humor in Czechoslovakia. *East Europe* 18, no. 4 (April): 27–28.
1969b Political Laughter in Poland. *East Europe* 18, no. 1 (January): 25–27.
1971 *Politiska Anekdoter från Osteuropa.* Stockholm: Utrikespolitiska Institutet.
1977 Mieux vaut en rire. *Vivre à l'Est. Les Temps Modernes,* 33:671, 714, 790, 850, 940.
1989a 'Chistes': Political Humor in Cuba. Washington: Cuban American National Foundation.
1989b The Joke Factory and the Wall. *New York Times,* 7 November 1989, 22.

Aranyossy, Georges
1971 *Ils ont tué ma foi.* Paris: Editions Robert Laffont.

Beckmann, Petr
1969 *Whispered Anecdotes:* Humor from Behind the Iron Curtain. Boulder: Golem Press.
1980 *Hammer and Tickle:* Clandestine Laughter in the Soviet Empire. Boulder: Golem Press. [Revised edition of *Whispered Anecdotes*]

Beezley, William H.
1985 Recent Mexican Political Humor. *Journal of Latin American Lore* 11:195–223.

Belgrader, Michael
1989 Review of *First Prize: Fifteen Years! Fabula* 30:111–12.

Benton, Greg, and Graham Loomes
1976 *Big Red Joke Book.* London: Pluto Press.

Benton, Gregor
1988 The Origins of the Political Joke. In Chris Powell and George E. C. Paton, eds., *Humour in Society: Resistance and Control.* London: Macmillan. 33–55.

172

Brandes, Stanley H.
 1977 Peaceful Protest: Spanish Political Humor in a Time of Crisis. *Western Folklore,* 36:331–46.

Brandt, Hans-Jürgen
 1965 *Witz mit Gewehr:* Bezieltes Lachen hinter Mauer und Stacheldraht. Stuttgart: Henry Goverts Verlag.

Bregman, Alexander
 1967 Poking Fun at Mao. *East Europe* 16, no. 3 (March): 21–22.

Brunvand, Jan Harold
 1973 'Don't Shoot, Comrades': A Survey of the Submerged Folklore of Eastern Europe. *North Carolina Folklore* 21:181–88.

Carnes, Pack
 1989 American Political Jokes: The Iranian Example. *Motif: International Newsletter of Research in Folklore and Literature* 9:3–7.

Čížek, Alois, and J. P. Morris
 1973 Humor Na Ně. Munich: CCC Books.

Cochran, Robert
 1989 'What Courage!' Romanian 'Our Leader' Jokes. *Journal of American Folklore,* 102:259–74.

Dallin, David J.
 1949 Told Behind the Iron Curtain. *New York Times Magazine,* 2 October 1949, 15.

Davies, Christie
 1981 Humor in Handcuffs. *Policy Review* 18:153–55.

Dolgopolova, Z.
 1982 *Russia Dies Laughing: Jokes from Soviet Russia.* London: Andre Deutsch.

Dor, Milo, and Reinhard Federmann
 1964 *Der Politische Witz.* Munich: Verlag Kurt Desch.

Draitser, Emil
 1978 *Forbidden Laughter* (Soviet Underground Jokes). Trans. Jon Pariser. Los Angeles: Almanac Publishing House.

Drozdzynski, Alexander
 1974 *Der politische Witz im Ostblock.* Düsseldorf: Droste Verlag.

Dundes, Alan
 1971 Laughter Behind the Iron Curtain: A Sample of Rumanian Political Jokes. *The Ukranian Quarterly* 27:50–59.

Durocher, Bruno
 1965 *La Guerre Secrète du Rire.* Paris: Editions Albin Michel.

Engel, Hans-Ulrich
 1984 *Nichts Neues an der finnisch-chinesischen Grenze.* Der politische Witz aus Osteuropa. Munich: Olzog.

Filip, Ota, and Ivan Steiger
 1977 *Schwejk heute: Politischer Witz in Prag.* Universitas Verlag.

Gamm, Hans-Jochen
 1979 *Der Flusterwitz in Dritten Reich.* Munich: Deutschen Taschenbuch. [First published in 1963]

García, P.
  1977 *Los chistes de Franco.* Madrid: C. Martínez Campos.
Harris, David A.
  1989 Defining a String Quartet, And Other Soviet Wisdom. *International Herald Tribune,* 11 October 1989, 9.
Harris, David A., and Izrail Rabinovich
  1988 *The Jokes of Oppression: The Humor of Soviet Jews.* Northvale, N.J.: J. Aronson.
Hellberg, Elena F.
  1985 [1987] 'The Other Way Round': The Jokelore of Radio Yerevan. *Arv:Scandinavian Yearbook of Folklore* 41:89–104.
Hirche, Kurt
  1964 *Der 'Braune' und der 'Rote' Witz.* Düsseldorf: Econ Verlag.
  1977 *West-östlicher Witzdiwan: 555 politische Witze.* Wien: Econ Verlag.
Isnard, Armand
  1977 *Raconte . . . Popov! Les histoires drôles de derrière le Rideau de fer.* Paris: Éditions Mengès.
Jacobi, Hermann
  1965 *Flusterwitze und Karikaturen aus dem Osten.* Bern: Verlag Schweizerisches Ost-Institut.
Kalbouss, George
  1977 On 'Armenian Riddles' and Their Offspring 'Radio Erevan.' *Slavic and East European Journal* 21:447–49.
Kalina, Ján L.
  1980 *Nichts zu lachen: Der politische Witz im Ostblock.* Munich: Herbig.
Kaplan, Robert D.
  1984 Rumanian Gymnastics. *New Republic* 191, no. 25 (December 17): 10, 12.
Katona, Imre
  1980 *Mi a különbség? Közéleti vicceinkröl.* Budapest: Magvetö Kiadó.
Kishtainy, Khalid
  1985 *Arab Political Humour.* London: Quartet Books.
Kolasky, John
  1972 *Look Comrade—The People Are Laughing: Underground Wit, Satire and Humour from Behind the Iron Curtain.* Ontario: Peter Martin Associates.
Kukin, Mischka
  1962 *Humor hinter dem Eisernen Vorhang.* Gütersloh: Signum Verlag.
Langnas, I. A.
  1963 Poland's Invisible Export. *East Europe* 12, no. 9 (September): 16–21.
Larsen, Egon
  1980 *Wit as a Weapon: The Political Joke in History.* London: Frederick Muller Ltd.
Levy, Alan
  1976 Poland's Polish Jokes. *New York Times,* 8 August 1976, section 6, 22–23, 25 27.

Lewis, Flora
   1956 Laughter Behind the Iron Curtain. *New York Times Magazine,*
       2 September 1956, 12.
Lo Bello, Nino
   1966 I Heard Jokes Behind the Iron Curtain. *The Catholic Digest* 30, no. 3
       (January): 23–26.
Luray, Martin
   1957 Bitter Wit from Hungary *New York Times,* 7 April 1957, section
       6, 16.
Lukes, Steven, and Itzhak Galnoor
   1985 *No Laughing Matter: A Collection of Political Jokes.* London:
       Routledge and Kegan Paul.
Lutfi al-Sayyid Marsot, Afaf
   1980 Humor: The Two-Edged Sword. *Middle East Studies Association
       Bulletin* 14, no. 1: 1–9.
Marzolph, Ulrich
   1988 Reconsidering the Iranian Sources of a Romanian Political Joke.
       Western Folklore 47: 212–16.
Mavrodin, Octavian
   1983 *Te Picipe Tine De Ris!* Colectie de Bancuri, vol. 1. Arhus: Nord.
Melor, Viloric
   1979 *L'arme du rire: L'humour dans les pays de l'Est.* Paris: Editions
       Ramsey.
Meyer, Antoine, and Philippe Meyer
   1978 *Le communisme est-il soluble dans l'alcool?* Paris: Editions du
       Seuil.
Michael, Wolfgang
   1974 *Radio Eriwans Nachtprogramm.* Frankfurt: Fischer Taschenbuch
       Verlag.
Mikes, George
   1971 *Any Souvenirs? Central Europe Revisited.* London: Andre Deutsch.
Nelan, Bruce W.
   1990 Rumania: Unfinished Revolution. *Time* 135, no. 2, 8 January 1990,
       28–34.
Olin, Nikolaj
   1970 *Govorit Radio Erevan.* Munich: Logos.
   1975 *Radio Erevan Prodolzhaet Govorit* [Radio Erevan Continues to
       Broadcast]. N.p.: Vamizdat.
Omidsalar, Mahmoud
   1987 A Romanian Political Joke in 12th Century Iranian Sources. *Western
       Folklore* 46: 121–24.
Orso, Ethelyn G.
   1979 *Modern Greek Humor.* Bloomington: Indiana University Press.
Parry, Albert
   1966 Russia Cracks Jokes about China. *New York Times Magazine,*
       26 June 1966, 14–15, 38, 41.

Parth, Wolfgang W., and Michael Schiff
  1972 *Neues von Radio Eriwan*. Frankfurt: Fischer Taschenbuch Verlag.
Paruit, Alain
  1978 *Les Barbelés de Rire: Humour politique dans les pays de l'est*. Paris: Editions Albatros.
Popescu, C. C.
  1985 *Te Picipe Tine De Ris!* Colectie de Bancuri, vol. 2. Arhus: Nord.
Radhayrapetian, Juliet
  1983 Political Humor: Its Function and Significance in the Iranian Revolution. *Folklore and Mythology Studies* 7:24–39.
Rafael, Vincente L.
  1986 Fishing, Underwear, and Hunchbacks: Humor and Politics in the Philippines, 1886 and 1983. *Bulletin of Concerned Asian Scholars* 18, no. 3:2–7.
Roberts, Edwin A., Jr.
  1966 Red Elephant Joke: Russia's Submerged River of Humor, *National Observer*, 26 September 1966, 1.
Röhrich, Lutz
  1977 *Der Witz*. Stuttgart: J. B. Metzler.
Ruksenas, Algis
  1986 *Is That You Laughing Comrade? The World's Best Russian (Underground) Jokes*. Secaucus, N.J.: Citadel Press.
Sanders, Jaquin
  1962 The Seriousness of Humor: Political Satire in the Soviet Bloc. *East Europe* 11, no. 1 (January): 21–29; 11, no. 2 (February): 23–27.
Schiff, Michael
  1969 *Radio Eriwan Antwortet*. Munich: Lichtenberg Verlag.
  1975 *Radio Eriwans Auslandsprogramm*. Frankfurt: Fischer Taschenbuch Verlag.
Shenker, Israel
  1978 U.S. Scholars Tickled Pink by Red Jokes. *New York Times*, 23 June 1978, 9.
Shturman, Dora, and Sergei Tictin
  1985 *Sovetskii Soiuz v zerkale politicheskogo anekdota*. London: Overseas Publications Interchange
Speier, Hans
  1975 *Witz und Politik: Essay uber die Macht und das Lachen*. Zürich: Edition Interfrom AG.
Steiger, Ivan
  1976 *Radio Eriwans Mattscheibe*. Frankfurt: Fischer Taschenbuch Verlag.
Stein, Mary Beth
  1989 The Politics of Humor: The Berlin Wall in Jokes and Graffiti. *Western Folklore* 48:85–108.
Streit, Peggy
  1964 Jokes That Seep Through the Iron Curtain. *New York Times Magazine*, 19 April 1964, 28, 56.

Sulzberger, C. L.
   1962 The Deadliest Radio of Them All. *New York Times,* 22 August 1962, 32.
   1964 Did You Ever See a Dog Walking? *New York Times,* 22 June 1964, 26.

Swearingen, Rodger
   1961 *What's So Funny, Comrade?* New York: Frederick A. Praeger.

Swoboda, Pawel
   1969 *Lach leiser, Genosse.* Zweite Folge. Munich and Esslingen: Bechtle Verlag.

Torgerg, Friedrich
   1967 Fug und Unfug des politicischen Witzes. *Der Monat* 19, no. 224 (May): 35–42.

Webber, Sabra J.
   1987 The Social Significance of the Cairene *Nukta:* Preliminary Observations. *Newsletter of the American Research Center in Egypt,* no. 138 (Summer): 1–10.

Westermarck, Edward
   1929 *Memories of My Life.* London: George Allen and Unwin.

Winick, Charles
   1964 *USSR Humor.* Mount Vernon, New York: Peter Pauper Press.

Wolfe, Bertram D.
   1951 Russian Jokes: Not Passed by the Censor. *New York Times,* 22 July 1951, section 6, 13.

Index